WRITERS AND THEIR WORK

ISOBEL ARMSTRONG
General Editor

BRYAN LOUGHREY
Advisory Editor

D0316373

ALAN AYCKBOURN

CPS 16588 5m 9/98

Tony Bartholomew

SIR ALAN AYCKBOURN

ALAN AYCKBOURN

MICHAEL HOLT

Northcote House
in association with the
British Council

© Copyright 1999 by Michael Holt.

First published in 1999 by Northcote House Publishers Ltd, Plymbridge House, Estover Road, Plymouth PL6 7PY, United Kingdom.
Tel: +44 (01752) 202368 Fax: +44 (01752) 202330.

British Library Cataloguing-in-Publication Data
A catalogue record for this book is available from the British Library

ISBN 0-7463-0859-0

Typeset by PDQ Typesetting, Newcastle-under-Lyme
Printed and bound in the United Kingdom

In memory of Trevor Smith

Contents

Acknowledgements

Anyone writing on Alan Ayckbourn is bound to be indebted to the two critics who have written with such insight about his work, Michael Billington and Albert E. Kalson. I am grateful for their infectious enthusiasm and perception. I must also thank David Moore, and a number of people at the Stephen Joseph Theatre in Scarborough for all the help given so generously: Jeannie Swales, Stephen Wood, the ever helpful Heather Stoney, and, of course, many thanks to Sir Alan Ayckbourn for so many terrific plays, conversations and production experiences.

Biographical Outline

1939   Born 12 April in Hampstead; father a violinist, mother a writer of romantic novels.

1946   Weekly boarder at local boarding school. Mother remarries a bank manager; lives at Billingshurst, Wisborough Green, Horsham, Uckfield, Hayward's Heath, and Lewes.

1951   Barclay's Bank scholarship to Haileybury School. Writes house plays; edits house magazine; tours Netherlands in school production of *Romeo and Juliet* (1955), and eastern USA and Canada in *Macbeth* (1956). Also 'quite good at cricket'.

1956–7 Leaves school with A levels in English and History. Acting assistant stage manager with Sir Donald Wolfit's production at Edinburgh Festival. Unpaid student assistant stage manager at Worthing with small walk-on parts. Then weekly rep in Leatherhead, summer season in Scarborough with Stephen Joseph, and winter season in Oxford as stage manager/actor.

1958–9 Works with the Stephen Joseph company at Scarborough for summer seasons at Library Theatre, touring to Stoke and elsewhere in winter.

1959   First two performed plays, *The Square Cat* and *Dad's Tale*, written under nom de plume Roland Allen. Marries Christine Allen – they have two sons and are separated some years later.

1960–63 Continues to write and perform at Scarborough Theatre-in-the-Round. Founder member and associate director of Victoria Theatre, Stoke-on-Trent, writes further plays including *Mr Whatnot*, and acts in repertoire.

1964	Joins BBC Radio at Leeds as drama producer, staying until 1970.
1965–9	Combines summer season work at Scarborough with BBC work. *Meet My Father*, retitled *Relatively Speaking* staged in London. Further plays follow, starting life in Scarborough and transferring to West End.
1970	Becomes director of productions at Scarborough.
1971–86	Continues to write plays for initial performance at Scarborough in Library Theatre and from 1976 at the Westwood Theatre. Most transfer to London stage and are performed internationally.
1986–7	Leaves Scarborough for two years to direct for the National Theatre Company in London. His production of *A View from the Bridge* transfers to the Aldwych Theatre and for it he receives Plays and Players Best Director (1987) award. Also receives Evening Standard Best Play award for his NT production of his own play *A Small Family Business*.
1987	Returns as director of productions to Scarborough, first to Westwood Theatre and then, following a Lottery Grant, to the refurbished Odeon Cinema, now the Stephen Joseph Theatre (1996).
1997	Marries Heather Stoney and is honoured with the title Sir Alan Ayckbourn.

1

Not Alan Ayckbourn

In *Anger and After* (1962), John Russell Taylor describes Alan Ayckbourn as 'a twenty three year old actor...whose play *Standing Room Only* showed more than promise, if less than complete achievement'. It might seem surprising that Alan Ayckbourn should be included in a survey of British play writing from 1956 to 1962, the period when English theatre discovered the kitchen sink and reinvigorated itself. In fact, this was his fourth professionally produced play, and was to be shortly followed by two others mounted in London's West End. Russell Taylor's influential book was a much admired critical survey but, even in its second edition in 1969, the judgement on Ayckbourn was unchanged – 'a less than complete achievement – the same might be said of his later West End comedy success *Relatively Speaking*'.

Ayckbourn is rarely linked with the generation of playwrights that included Osborne, Wesker, Arden, Pinter and Delaney. But he started writing in 1959 at the time when the new wave of writers was just emerging and, indeed, many of them shared Margaret Ramsey as literary agent. Ayckbourn was alarmed at a party to see several of his fellow young literary bloods wearing badges saying 'I am not Alan Ayckbourn'. Clearly this young playwright was already deemed an outsider and for much of his career he suffered from a critical prejudice that it took many plays written over many years to shake.

It is easy to see why he was dismissed so early on. The cultural revolution that followed *Look Back in Anger* pursued its own theatrical orthodoxy. The old theatre establishment – its playwrights and actors, its subject matter and audience, its commercial and management structure – was viewed with great suspicion. Alan Ayckbourn did not fit easily into the new order.

Neither he nor his characters had an overtly political agenda. His plays were not set in a working-class environment; indeed, they clearly described middle-class settings and preoccupations. Most suspicious of all, he apparently aspired to writing 'well made' plays and was promising to have great commercial potential. Resolutely sticking to comedy as his chosen genre, he quickly found star actors and managements eager to snap up his plays. It seems all too obvious that, in the cultural climate of the 1960s, he would be labelled as the inheritor of the lightweight boulevardier mantle recently worn by Terence Rattigan, Peter Ustinov and Enid Bagnold.

But he never claimed this role; success in London's West End did not lure him to the capital. He obstinately chose to remain living and working in Scarborough, a small holiday town nestling between two bays remote on the Yorkshire coast. He has lived there for most of the past twenty-five years, writing and directing fifty-two plays for a tiny theatre company of which he is artistic director. The majority of these plays have been premiered in Ayckbourn's seaside playhouse and produced in the West End one or two years later. They cover a variety of genres and comic styles with an ever expanding thematic base. His challenging of the dramatic unities through experiments with time and chance have continually defied expectations of both audiences and critics. Each play has found commercial and critical success throughout the world; each has chipped away at the prejudice born in the early sixties.

It might be tempting to see Ayckbourn's remarkable achievements as his response to the early labelling of him as unfashionably orthodox. It would be a mistake to do so, for in both subject matter and accomplishment, this playwright has stuck resolutely to his theatrical roots. It is difficult to overestimate the influence on his work of the Theatre-in-the-Round established by Stephen Joseph in Scarborough in the 1950s. It provided him with his early training, opportunities and principles. Throughout his international success, it has made artistic demands on him as a director and as resident playwright. He continues to provide it with new work and has a gallery of new writers there under his tutelage.

It was in 1957 that Alan Ayckbourn first went to Scarborough as an actor/assistant stage manager and general factotum to the theatre's director. Stephen Joseph was the son of actress Hermione Gingold and Michael Joseph the publisher, and was to play a large part in the evolution of Alan Ayckbourn the playwright. It was under him that the first attempts to write for the theatre were made. The first six plays were written to commission and through them Ayckbourn developed the technical skill which was to stand him in such good stead. It is worthwhile charting the course of this process. It reveals a young artist intent on learning his craft within the context of an active theatre. He was fortunate to find himself under the inspiration and guidance of an experienced if idiosyncratic theatre director

Stephen Joseph was a charismatic personality who stimulated a whole generation of theatre makers with his furiously espoused enthusiasms. Forming ad hoc companies housed wherever he could find a venue, Joseph promoted a sort of popular, vital theatre, perhaps best typified by his idea for a 'Fish and Chip Theatre', where actors would have to compete with a chip shop and an audience free to move around the auditorium.

This venture never came to fruition. But he did establish a summer company in a room above the Public Library in Scarborough. There, his enthusiastic but underpaid acting company was also expected to have other skills to be called upon if necessary. They would often be asked to act as technicians and, if they showed any interest, encouraged to write plays for performance to the audience of holidaymakers and seaside landladies. These new playwrights were thus technically knowledgeable and audience-aware.

At the heart of Joseph's work was an espousal of the theatre-in-the-round form of staging. He had encountered this in the USA at Dallas, Houston and Fort Worth and became its most vigorous champion in this country. His advocacy of arena theatre emphasized the inexpensive nature of design for its productions, always a concern for Joseph with his shoestring finances.

Outsiders such as John Russell Taylor saw it as the ideal vehicle for the encouraging of new writing; low production overheads, they reasoned, emphasized the quality of the script. It was true that Joseph was very dedicated to new writing; he had a great skill in seeing exactly where a script succeeded and where its dramatic potential could be developed. The Scarborough

3

company had promoted the careers of David Campton, Peter Terson, James Saunders and Harold Pinter.

But it was not really economic factors that excited Stephen Joseph about the arena configuration. The actor's relationship with the audience was the prime concern. Theatre-in-the-round unified actor and audience in one shared theatrical volume. With the audience seated all around them, the actors and their skills are fully exposed. Take away the barrier of a proscenium arch, Joseph argued, and the spectator is confronted with the three-dimensional reality of an actor's presence. And when no architectural shield exists between actor and audience, the actor must 'be' rather than rely on performing. Truth in the acting is a prime requirement when actor and audience are in such close proximity. It can be very vivid for the audience and this is achieved very often on the Scarborough stage. Many stories are told about the consequences. During a performance of *The Norman Conquests*, the actor playing the character Tom was greeted by a man in the front row saying 'Eeh, here's Tom, now! Come on in, Lad'.

It is one of many stories born out of the close physical relationship between willing spectator and truthful actor. But Stephen Joseph rejected the description of theatre-in-the-round as 'intimate'. He recognized the danger in the term. He wrote, 'It is not a word I like in this context. It implies a domestic, if passionate, relationship while I want to emphasise a theatrical relationship in which there shall be passion indeed' (*New Theatre Forms*, 1968).

Clearly he did not want the audience ever to lose the other effect proximity to the actor can evoke, an acute theatricality. The arena stage form invites an awareness of the actor as player. Just a few feet away from where they sit, the audience sees both a real person and an assumed identity. The essence of acting, personification, is in this dichotomy of real person and false character. That implied duality is heightened when, denied spectacular scenic effects and elaborate properties, the audience is confronted with what the actor alone can provide. They become especially aware of the artificiality, of seeing a real person, close enough to be almost within arm's reach, pretending to be a different 'real' person.

Theatre-in-the-round involves a particular awareness of the

interplay of truth and artifice. It is a twin concern which is at the centre of all drama, but particularly useful to the comic writer. It is present on all stages, but particularly effective in the round.

And these two elements lie at the heart of Alan Ayckbourn's plays. He is at once concerned to present his audience with recognizably real characters in 'true' situations and also to enjoy the anomalies of theatrical convention. Some of Ayckbourn's best explorations of the consequences of upsetting theatrical conventions come unstuck when translated into the proscenium arch. *Taking Steps* (1979), for instance, is so dependent on the audience seeing the whole map of the stage that it has yet to find a completely satisfactory production behind a proscenium arch. In Scarborough, where the audience is sitting all around and able to comprehend the map, the play is incredibly, painfully funny. It is a comedy born out of the audience's conspiracy with the actor to ignore Aristotelian unity of space.

At the same time, the grotesquely self-obsessed characters are recognizably truthful pictures of humanity, especially when played, as in the original production, with transparent honesty. One has met many a bombast like Roland, innumerable ruthless careerists like Lizzie, and at least one Tristram.

Ken Boden, theatre manager from the beginning of the Scarborough venture alongside first Joseph and later Ayckbourn, confided, 'You know who that Tristram really is, don't you? That's Alan Ayckbourn when he first started here...perfect picture of him as a young lad.' It is entirely believable; even today, the world's most successful comic dramatist is painfully shy, finding it difficult to make direct eye contact with all but the closest of friends and confidants. It is hard to square this with the aspiring, moderately successful young actor who arrived in 1957 to join the company, until one remembers how acting is often a refuge for the sensitive and timid personality.

The Library Company which this shy teenager joined, played summer seasons in Scarborough and toured venues throughout the Midlands during the winter. In 1958, Ayckbourn complained of the lightweight role of Nicky that he had been assigned to play in John van Druten's comedy *Bell, Book, and Candle*. 'If you want a better part, you'd better write one yourself', was Stephen Joseph's characteristic reply. 'Write a play, I'll do it. If it's any good.'

The Square Cat (1959) was the result of this challenge and it was first performed the next summer. It was written, like all of Alan Ayckbourn's first plays, under the name of Roland Allen, a mixture of his own and his wife's names. Subtitled *A Cool Comedy*, its plot hangs on the idea that a repressed middle-aged wife, Alice Glover, makes a secret assignation with a young rock and roll star called Jerry Wattis, at the home of an absent second cousin. She, poor infatuated soul, desires no more than to dance with her idol; he has other, though less clearly specified, ambitions for his meeting with what he thinks is a young, single woman.

Alice's husband and her rugby player son turn up and are suitably outraged and obstructive until they realize that the real personality behind the pop star image is a shy, bespectacled figure of dry respectability. They can now enjoy the tables turned on mum's fantasy, until, that is, the schizoid hero reappears as a rockin', guitar strummin', clearly potent, sex symbol. The plot thickens when the daughter of the family, Susan, falls in love with the pop star's demure alter-ego (real name Arthur Brummage). The play's final act has Jerry Wattis chased out of the house by angry husband wielding a battle axe, mum lying drunk on the sofa. Susan, clearly unaware of the duality of his personality, announces the arrival of her fiancé and introduces the family to – of course – Arthur Brummage!

'Unashamedly (and rather foolishly) I had given myself the lion's share of everything... quite apart from singing, dancing and playing the guitar – none of which I could do – I had all the laugh lines and got the girl – well, two actually!' says Ayckbourn. However, self-promoting though it might be, the script shows quite remarkable talent for a first play by a 19-year old author.

It is neatly constructed, and, once the basic premise is accepted, it skilfully rises to frenetic climaxes and frantic farcical scenes as Jerry Wattis transforms into Arthur Brummage both onstage and off. It demonstrates that the young author already has a clear grasp of comedy arising out of character and situation. The comic dialogue is situation led – 'Your mother is one of those lucky people who never grew up. The unlucky ones are those who have to live with her.' It is peppered with the idiosyncratic word jokes that are the hallmark of later plays. When told he cannot meet the rock star, the father complains,

'Lots of people have unhappy childhoods – mine was hell! But that doesn't make me allergic to husbands.' Above all, it revels in its own theatricality and particularly in the dramatic possibilities of role switching.

Nonetheless, it is clearly a product of its time, reading like a boulevard comedy of the kind that the West End clung to for the next twenty years in the plays of William Douglas Home. The characters are classic types from this genre – the scatty middle-aged wife, the bombastic husband, the sporty son and the 'soubrette' daughter. Its three-act structure, though very skilfully orchestrated, seems old-fashioned. It is just the sort of play that people were to assume that Alan Ayckbourn wrote, especially if they had never seen any of his later work.

But from the start they were wrong. *The Square Cat* was only the first of four plays by Roland Allen which were mounted at Scarborough and its sister theatre at Stoke-on-Trent. They were all very different in style and intention; through them, Alan Ayckbourn learned the craft of play writing. It is illuminating to examine them for the range and development they cover and for the seeds of themes and characters that were to emerge later more fully realized. However, they must be pieced together from anecdote, photographs and newspaper reviews. Some scripts are missing and others only reluctantly brought out.

In the winter of 1959, *Love After All* was a reworking of *The Barber of Seville*, but this script is no longer in existence, though some photographs of the production show the author acting in four further disguises. There were two versions of the play, one modern and one Edwardian, and of it Ayckbourn says 'Stephen Joseph warned me that the second [play] was going to be a lot harder but, because I stole the plot of this it was actually a lot easier. It was about a very handsome young man – played of course by the author – wooing and winning the beautiful but brainless heroine...The finale had several Chinamen rushing about. Heaven knows why. The Guardian described it as "lacking in wit".'

Dad's Tale (1960), which was based on Mary Norton's classic children's novel *The Borrowers*, involved sections of dance drama and the same action described from several different perspectives. It was perhaps over-ambitious but it was produced in December 1960 and, Ayckbourn recalls, 'It was my first children's show. It opened in Scarborough just before Christmas and, including the director, played to an audience of five with an average age of forty. It was my first taste of theatrical failure.'

However, *Standing Room Only* (1961) was, he says, 'quite a step forward for me as a writer'. Prompted by Stephen Joseph's wish to do a play about overpopulation, but ignoring his suggestion that it be set on Venus, Ayckbourn gives us a traffic jam on Shaftesbury Avenue. It is 1997 ('which seemed a very long way away at the time') and there is a permanent traffic standstill from London to Birmingham. Passes are required by law to move anywhere away from your vehicle, which compounds Nita's problem. Not having passed her Maternity Exam, she is illegally pregnant, and has to have the outlawed baby delivered secretly in her home. This is a traffic-jammed, double-decker bus, and it also houses her obstreperous pa and pompous fiancé. The exploration of overpopulation becomes merely a comic background to other themes. Ayckbourn is once again focused on family relationships, with an essentially optimistic sense that stranded humanity will survive come what may. They will not, it is true, be living in perfect harmony, for even though it has an Absurdist situation as the basis for the plot, the play explores a theme that was to be revisited in a number of later plays. The menfolk breeze through the compound difficulties of the baby's delivery with a feigned normality that shrugs off the emotional discomfort of all around them. They take refuge from it by concentrating on the mechanics of everyday life, such as secret codes on the bus's bell and systems to pass buckets of hot water for the baby's delivery.

Though 'optioned' by a successful management, *Standing Room Only* never made the West End. *Mr Whatnot* (1963) did, though it received short shrift from the critics. They found its over-glossy London production too whimsical. It is a play that revels in its own theatricality. At Scarborough, the contrivance, central to the play, of miming most props to an accompanying sound effect must have seemed a natural device. In the round, any large prop is likely be rejected as too big for some part of the audience to look over or too expensive for a seaside rep to acquire. A piano tuner striking chords from an invisible pianoforte or a starting handle being turned on an indiscernible car are part of this theatre's usual vocabulary. Ayckbourn senses the essential theatricality arising out of this limitation and exploits the device to the full in *Mr Whatnot*.

Aware of the implicit absurdity of the convention, he peoples his play with a cast of grotesques. The Slingsby-Craddocks are a cartoon upper-crust family – chinless, brainless and gutless. They are barely able to communicate with each other or their silent butler, and when they do it is in staccato cliché. Discovering his piano is flat, Lord Slingsby-Craddock phones a piano tuner, whom the programme, if not the dialogue, reveals as Mint. This strange personality never speaks but communicates entirely through mime. A bit of a problem on the telephone you might think, but the young dramatist is by now very assured. With a one-sided bit of telephone dialogue, Ayckbourn deftly manages to get Mint to the stately home, where he tunes the piano, plays tennis, and falls in love with the daughter of the family.

He does this, unable to communicate his name to anyone, including the audience. Onstage he is referred to as 'Mr Whatnot' and he is an extraordinary invention. He is wild, absurd, anarchic and irreverent. He would be at home in the *Goon Show* and has many of the touching qualities of Charlie Chaplin or Buster Keaton. In the tennis match, he is so desperate to beat the daughter's fiancé and prove himself that he cheats ruthlessly. Perhaps the abiding image is of Jacques Tati's Monsieur Hulot, another victim, even in a tennis match, to inanimate objects. For Mint is a true victim of technology, be it as simple as a dripping tap or as complex as a truculent motor car. Like Hulot, faced with the niceties of over-polite behaviour, he has trouble with the cutlery, the soup and the drink. His vulnerability and his madcap solutions to these situations are at once logical and hilariously preposterous. In all of this, Mint is both understandable and endearing. We are offered no explanation as to who he is or why he is as he is, and certainly he is at odds with the precious environment of the stately home. It is his dramatic function to create havoc, because he is a misfit, a stranger with no evil intent, who undermines the social situation he finds himself in. It is a plot line which we will see developed many times in the course of Ayckbourn's subsequent writing.

As a stage creation, Mint is as far away from the world of *The Square Cat* as it is possible to imagine. But then so are the

Slingsby-Craddocks. They are each, in their own way, exaggerated cartoons of Ayckbourn's first family of characters. They are a jibe at the archetypal family that belonged to the world of West End comedies in the 1950s. The London theatre had reflected the privileged world of a sophisticated upper class and its rural values. The comedy of manners to be seen on Shaftesbury Avenue between the wars and into the mid 1960s still reflected prewar society unaffected by the socialist government of 1945 and the inroads of the welfare state. At the time when Alan Ayckbourn was developing his skills as a young playwright, this theatrical vision was being swept from the British theatre's stages by the revolution that Russell Taylor describes in *Anger and After*. New playwrights with new agendas scorned the values of the West End audience they had inherited, preferring to seek new audiences from a different class.

Ayckbourn was linked early on with the old guard because his next play after *Mr Whatnot* had the kind of success that West End managements had always cherished. *Relatively Speaking* (1967) was a triumph, both critically and commercially, when it was taken from Scarborough, where its title had been *Meet My Father*, to the Duke of York's Theatre in London. It is a play which starts the playwright's investigation into the world of his audience.

For the irony is that whilst the 'Anger' playwrights sought new audiences from the class that continued to find the cinema and television its natural media, Ayckbourn wrote plays for the next twenty years which described the values, concerns and angst of the emerging lower middle class. This was the theatre's natural audience throughout the latter half of the twentieth century. An increasingly wealthy, mobile, articulate, educated society found in his plays descriptions of their own lives, personalities from their own environment, problems from their own experience.

The socialist playwrights sought 'relevance' to their desired audience but turned increasingly to historical metaphor or to the depiction of working-class guilt in an Oxbridge environment. Ayckbourn had no such agenda or guilt. His approach had been defined in Scarborough. 'Stephen Joseph asked me...for a play which would make people laugh when their seaside summer holidays were spoiled by the rain and they came into the theatre to get dry before trudging back to their

10

landladies. It seemed to me as worthwhile a reason for writing a play as any, so I tried to comply. I hope I have succeeded.'

There is here the concealment that conspired to build for Ayckbourn the reputation of a mere boulevardier. He has perpetually shown a reluctance to discuss or even acknowledge the deeper thrust of his plays, always insisting on an audience-centred purpose inherited from Stephen Joseph. His success in appealing to that audience can be judged by the way in which theatre managements both nationally and internationally came to rely upon his output as the mainstay of their theatre's offerings. The popular success they guaranteed was so secure that critic Robin Thornber was to describe Ayckbourn as 'the man who saved the British theatre'. Such popular success always breeds suspicion in intellectual minds; popular success, they can be heard saying, cannot be accompanied by intellectual value. And he only writes comedy.

But Ayckbourn is a great writer who transcends subject matter and genre. He produces great drama by observing the lives of those holidaymakers and their landladies. His subjects are mostly ordinary upper-working- or middle-class people living in small-town communities, struggling to fit into small-time morality, afloat on a sea of problems largely of their own making. The plays are all uproariously funny and therefore attract that holiday audience. They are also accurate and, in that accuracy, painfully bleak, dark and tragic.

It is only possible to deal with a handful of them in a short book like this, but by sampling them in more or less chronological order, we can chart the progress of a playwright dismissed at first as being focused on the wrong class, using the wrong techniques, with a wrong basic attitude and choosing the wrong genre. Alan Ayckbourn was not to be a playwright of the generation described by John Russell Taylor. However, it became increasingly clear that if he could not be categorized as a member of the kitchen sink brigade, nor was he easily dismissible as a simple exponent of the well made play.

2

Relative and Other Values

In *Relatively Speaking* (1965) there is a moment of sublime confusion which typifies the play and points to the thematic base beneath its glittering surface. Unfaithful husband Phillip thinks that Greg is his wife's lover and that he wants to marry her. But Greg is really the new boyfriend of Phillip's own ex-mistress, who announces that she has had a proposal of marriage. Phillip says 'Infectious this marriage epidemic. I seem to be the only one who's developed immunity'.

We are at once given a snapshot of the entire play and of the agenda which was to form the basis of the Ayckbourn canon. The relationships between men and women and the particular strains which the process and state of marriage inflict are the subject matter of the plays. Whatever the unfortunate Phillip thinks he is immune to, he is inevitably to be confounded. In Ayckbourn's plays, no one is immune to marriage or at least to the pursuit of the conjoining of man and woman. To imagine that you can be safe is foolish; individuals married or single are open to ambush by predatory individuals in pursuit of marital bliss or desperate to escape its clutches.

We do, however, encounter unmarried couples in this comic world who have just met and are in the initial throes of love or lust. In *Relatively Speaking* we first meet Greg and Ginny together in her Chelsea flat. They are clearly lovers and he has asked her to marry him; innocent young love preparing for a happy future. But lurking, quite literally, under the bed is the worm in this love apple.

Greg finds a pair of slippers there, not his own, and not, despite Ginny's feeble suggestion, the property of the pet dog. The poor young man is too besotted to tumble to the notion that they might have been left behind by another lover, and that this might explain the innumerable bunches of flowers in the bathroom. Indeed, he is so infatuated, he believes her story that she is setting out to visit her parents, and decides to follow her. But he will not only arrive at Ginny's parents home to ask for her hand in marriage; he will fall into one of Ayckbourn's suburban traps. Ginny's real errand is to break off from her previous sexual partner, Phillip, an older married man, and demand the return of incriminating letters.

Once again, a shy, socially inexperienced intruder blunders into the dangerous milieu of suburban married respectability. Arriving unannounced, Greg meets first, not Phillip, the unfaithful middle-aged husband, but his wife, Sheila, whom Greg takes to be his girlfriend's mother. His tongue-tied shyness and her English suburban manners invite lack of communication. 'No Ginny?' he asks. 'No I'm afraid not...' says Sheila, who is unaware of her supposed daughter, '...There's some sherry, if you'd like.'

The confusion is compounded by the arrival of Ginny. Thus we have the meeting of two couples: one legally married and one hoping to be. They are each made up of an innocent partner and one with a guilty past. The majority of the play is a hilarious journey through the pitfalls of misunderstandings when innocence meets guilt within the context of marriage and courtship. It is a structure that Ayckbourn was to exploit in many guises throughout his work.

In this early play, the action and the outcome are relatively sunny. Deceit is the mainspring of the plot. It is initiated by Ginny, though she might be forgiven her fibs to Greg as she sets out to do the right thing. Sheila tells whoppers too; she suspects her husband of philandering and has invented a lover by sending letters to herself. Sheila's game of deception, devised to deflect the cruelty of her husband's suspected adultery, is a comic counterpoint to Ginny's and it keeps the action going. Phillip only half believes in her affair. 'I mean, of the two people who live in this house, you are the only one who ever gets letters on Sunday. I mean, on a Sunday – who ever heard of letters on a Sunday?' What fun when this man, himself an arch deceiver, is introduced to a fresh faced young man who has apparently come to ask for his wife's hand in marriage.

Throughout the whole action there is never a moment when

Phillip, or Greg, or Sheila can be sure which of the four
characters know who is in what state of sexual or marital liaison.
Ayckbourn manages, with the most thorough use of dramatic
irony in any English comedy, to keep the two couples guessing
for the entire play who wants, or loves or has bedded whom.
Confusion piles upon confusion until the older couple are
waving goodbye to the youngsters. The outcome is relatively
upbeat. The new lovers leave, clutching each other and those
incriminating letters, seemingly heading towards some sort of
happiness; the old couple look as if they will continue their state
of uneasy mistrust.

However, the play finishes with some twenty lines that are
breathtaking in the way they threaten and overturn the
comfortable comic conclusion. Watching the young couple
leave, Sheila says 'Quite wrong for each other of course. It'll be
a disastrous marriage but great fun for them while it lasts'. She
casts a shadow over our happy ending, for we suspect that her
cynical assessment may be right. She is after all speaking from
bitter personal experience. And her remarks are given a very
cruel ring when Phillip discovers that the slippers found under
Ginny's bed are not his after all. Could it be that Ginny has
cruelly deceived everyone and that poor Greg is as cheated upon
as Phillip was? It is a black moment indeed. But the audience is
scarcely given the chance to digest its unpleasant implications.

'I was just wondering how that poor boy was going to make
out,' says Sheila. 'Never mind that...Whose are these?'
demands the deceived deceiver, in a penultimate line that
almost darkens the play beyond comedy. Magically, Ayckbourn
rescues the mood with a sprightly final rejoinder from the
cheated wife – 'Wouldn't you like to know!'

It is a line that demonstrates a young author's considerable
skill. It salts the wound of the unfaithful husband, and gives
triumph to the guiltless wife in as piquant a final line as any in
comedy. But it also makes one fear for the innocent in the other
relationship; will guileless Greg discover the other 'other' man,
and what will be *his* technique for dealing with the pain of
cuckoldry? This is a comic ending with the harsh foreboding of
truth attached to it. It does not have the bleak cruelty of such
moments in later plays. However, Ayckbourn's effect of counter-
pointing the potentially heartbreaking with the irresistibly comic

is germinated here. Such impeccable dramatic technique is something rare and was a source of pride to the author.

Ayckbourn tends to describe *Relatively Speaking* as an exercise in the 'well made play' – 'I think this is important for a playwright to do at least once in his life since, as in any science, he cannot begin to shatter theatrical convention or break golden rules until he is reasonably sure in himself what they are and how they were arrived at.' He had clearly learned well; with a great deal of Congreve on his bookshelves, it is no surprise that this play has the construction of a classic comedy. It divides into two parts; a short exposition, for all the world like a front-cloth scene, introducing us to the situation, followed by a longer exploitation of the comic complications arising from it.

The problem for both author and actor is how to make that first scene humorous and engaging as well as informative. It is not very easy; though Ayckbourn uses innumerable devices, comedy slippers, filling the stage with flowers sent by Phillip and a cheeky ironic mock-discovery of infidelity. It needs a very skilful comic actor to enlarge upon the stage directions and be sufficiently charming to capture the audience's sympathy. In the first West End production Richard Briers fulfilled this task superbly, but in a lesser actor's hands the writing in this opening scene can seem thin, too reliant on stage directions, and over-plotted.

Nonetheless, *Relatively Speaking*, with its superb comic complications, won its author national and international recognition. In this first success, we discover the nascent themes and techniques he was to use later. The surroundings are typically middle-class suburban, placed firmly, despite the author's home base, in the south of England. The hero is a shy young man, ill at ease in these unfamiliar surroundings. He causes mayhem almost accidentally through his gauche ineptness. This is reinforced by the behaviour of the other characters as they observe the social niceties of English middle-class politeness. The victim of his destructive presence is frequently the relationship of a married couple and, typically in *Relatively Speaking*, the marriage contains an innocent and a guilty party.

For Ayckbourn most relationships contain abuser and abused. A sample of his plays, following his first West End success, will show that his dramatic world is populated by them. As the plays

15

appear through the next ten years, these characters grow increasingly cruel and vulnerable. They are rarely truly evil and rarely completely innocent. Often they cause suffering by default, by neglect, or by the careless use of a defence mechanism. They are nearly always driven by emotional necessity. The picture drawn is of a battleground where the struggle is unending, truces are mostly temporary, and any happy peacetime a fleeting illusion. Marriage is not necessarily the cause of the abusive situation. But marriage is the structure that reinforces the difficulties inherent in the understanding of any partner.

In Ayckbourn's world, the married state itself frequently becomes a weapon of destruction – and not only for the husband or wife. For when marriages break down, they rarely implode. Marriage difficulties distribute their own disturbance; and as Kalson, the American critic who is particularly incisive about the themes, so aptly puts it, we get picture upon picture of 'the destruction caused by the fall-out from a disintegrating nuclear family'.

This is perhaps most clearly explored in the next West End success, *How the Other Half Loves* (1969). As the lights come up, we see two living rooms – 'Not a composite setting but two rooms contained and overlapping in the same area'. The Fosters have smart reproduction furniture in a tidy and neat household, but it shares the stage space with the trendy, modern but grubby fixtures of the Phillips's untidy home. Most graphically, the three-seater sofa is shared: two-seats Foster, (plump-cushioned Waring and Gillow), and one-seat Phillips (abused Habitat with children's toys under the cushions).

The dramatic purpose of this device is quickly explained. Fiona Foster telephones her younger lover, Bob Phillips. But when his wife, Teresa, answers, Fiona puts down the receiver and attends to the jaunty eccentricities of Frank, her own husband and Bob's employer. The two households are obviously once again connected by infidelity. This time, however, the action takes place within a setting that is a metaphor for the predicament of the adulterer.

The situation and the set, composed as they are of elements from two homes, look precarious. The threat of collapse is heightened when another marriage is dragged into it. William

Featherstone is also employed by Frank, and Bob uses him in a spur of the moment alibi to explain his own absence from home. He was, he claims, offering Featherstone advice about his wife's adultery. Almost simultaneously, Fiona is using Mary Featherstone as her alibi, saying that she has been advising her about handling William's extramarital affair. When the unfortunate Featherstones are invited to dinner, they become the victims of the deceit and confusion inherent in the situation. The result, of course, is to aggravate whatever cracks may have lurked under the surface of their own marriage. They suffer the domino effect of marital breakdown. But not before they have been socially and physically abused at dinner parties within both errant households.

Once again the setting provides the springboard for the comic action. Though they happen on two different nights, we see both dinner parties taking place simultaneously. The Featherstones switch from one table to another by simply swivelling their chairs, transcending both location and time. They become embroiled in embarrassingly vigorous rows between man and wife on two separate occasions. The fun is that we see them coping concurrently with the consequences.

Ayckbourn exploits the device to its full comic potential. At the Phillips' table, the Featherstones endeavour to be a calming influence patching the troubled marriage; at the Fosters', they try to make a good impression with William's boss and his impressive wife. Their efforts are of course doomed. Not only are they themselves suspected, on both occasions, of sexual indiscretion, William ends up covered in soup from a tureen thrown by Teresa. The hilarity of this humiliation is tinged by the suspicion amongst the audience that the playwright has snookered himself. How to explain a wet actor in the other household? Of course the technical wizard, Ayckbourn, has the coup waiting; Featherstone's humiliation is completed. He has been sitting under the leaking upstairs loo.

Despite such brilliant use of the split-location setting, this play is carried by more than just technical skill. The plotting and action are sustained by other dramatic elements; what happens is funny because of who it happens to. *How the Other Half Loves*, even more than *Relatively Speaking*, is underpinned by comic characterization. The three couples are drawn with a vivid observation that wittily individualizes every character and contrasts very different marital relationships.

The play starts with the morning routines of two households, the Phillips and the Fosters, juxtaposed on stage, dramatically and physically. So, from the start of the action, the way each couple treat each other in their early habits reflects the class differences between the marriages and explains the contrasting styles of loving.

The Fosters are the most well off of the couples, childless it seems, and have developed the decorous good manners of the sophisticated middle class. Even under stress they treat each other with polite, evasive insult. In this atmosphere an enquiry about suspected infidelity is posed with studied casualness. And it is parried with offers of 'more coffee' and the exchange of small gifts and shows of gratitude. It is an atmosphere in which toilet paper is referred to with discreet gentility – 'Darling! Crisis! We're out of bathroom stationery!'

In contrast, the Phillips live in a mess, engendered by baby Benjamin and Teresa's habit of cutting out *Guardian* articles for her own haphazard filing system scattered throughout the living room. It is a home where people inevitably tread on abandoned squeaky toys and leave coffee cups around. It is also an environment which invites a spiky, ill-tempered, confrontational relationship. Candid truths and physical objects alike are hurled for routine argument's sake, and an unfaithful husband is naturally over-defensive to the point of aggression when questioned about late homecoming. Inevitably he will seek to blame others, and who better than the Featherstones.

They are at the bottom of this social heap. William Featherstone is very anxious for professional advancement and his focus is almost entirely on impressing Frank Foster as the key to this. Mary is shy, gauche, even less socially experienced, and at the mercy of her husband's ambitious nature. He sees her as a necessary appendage and one which must be bullied into appropriate social skills. 'Do you realise, Mrs Foster, the hours I have put into that woman?' he cries in a remark that is as cruelly revealing of his marriage as it is of his farcical self-importance. When he is forced to stumble an apology to Mary, she exposes his real humiliation by saying, 'It's difficult for him. He's never been wrong before, you see.'

Each of the six partners is drawn with acute observation, not just for comic function but to underline the consequences of casual adultery upon them. Their relationships, Ayckbourn suggests, are shaped by character, and also by class grouping. The social armour you do or do not have is consequent upon financial position, educational background and emotional training.

Alan Ayckbourn is not a political didacticist, but it is hard to ignore the use of class differences in his plays. They are never presented with a political badge attached, for he is instinctively drawn to the underdog in whatever class he or she may be. But he does describe the consequences of being that underdog in different social circumstances. Ronald Bryden is therefore partially right when he says, '[Ayckbourn] is a political propagandist who works on people's minds without letting them know he's doing it or drawing attention to his own rectitude. He simply demonstrates in terms audiences have to recognise as fact, the tragic absurdity of some of the things our society forces on human beings.' But, for Ayckbourn, class is not imposed on his characters; it is a conspiracy they enter into. Bryden was writing this in his *Plays and Players* review of *Absurd Person Singular* (1972). This play, which won international acclaim on both sides of the Atlantic and throughout the world, is perhaps the most thorough working of this theme.

Significantly and typically, Ayckbourn chooses to demonstrate its cruel effects at Christmas, the mandatory jolly season, with its round of parties given for family, friends and professional colleagues. The six people we meet on three consecutive Christmases are joined more by professional ambition or obligation than by any deep friendship. True, there are hints of an adulterous relationship between Marion, the bank manager's wife, and Geoffrey, an architect with more sexual libido than professional expertise, but the three couples have become acquainted through business. It is clear from the start that Ronald and Marion are afforded the traditional status and respect that banking confers, even from the promising professional, Geoffrey and his wife Eva, whose emotional grasp is already crumbling in the face of her husband's suspected philandering.

Deference reaches ludicrous heights in the Hopcrofts. Sidney is an ambitious small-time property developer and Jane, another cowed wife who finds function and solace in being obsessively

19

houseproud. They are the Featherstones writ large, and it is to their spotless kitchen that we make our first Christmas visit. Ayckbourn deliberately chooses this room because it is 'back-stage' at the Christmas party. There is far more comedy, he insists, offstage than on. The social mask is most likely to be dropped here and the true picture of the occasion revealed.

And it is. Sidney is driving Jane hard in a frenzy of nervous anticipation, insisting on creating the proper impression with the important people at the party. If truth be told, he and his wife are clearly more at ease with Dick and Lottie Potter, two noisy guests we never meet since they stay in the living room. But they are not the 'useful' professionals that the occasion is planned to impress, with its carefully worked out timetable. Of course it all falls apart when these people arrive – 'Nineteen: twenty seven! They're early!!' – and Marion is performing with consummate ease. She declares the spotlessly tidy kitchen as 'dishy' without the trace of implied irony, and Sidney's do-it-yourself fittings are purred over as 'gorgeous', 'enchanting'. The washing machine is similarly hailed as an astounding techno-logical marvel, and the Hopcrofts never suspect they are being patronized. When the hosts' backs are turned, however, it is clear that Marion has set a time limit on attendance.

Ronald is clearly not interested in discussing banking at the party even though Sidney tries to ingratiate himself with his ugly property-dealer philosophy about 'dog eat dog' and 'you scratch my back and I'll scratch yours'. He should take lessons from Geoffrey's more skilled manipulation which, to Sidney's prudish working-class horror, includes dirty stories.

The comic climax is occasioned by Hopcroft's refusal to let his wife into the house after she has dashed out to the off-licence to get tonic for the gin. Rather than be disgraced by her appearance in a rain-sodden old mackintosh and slouch hat, he locks her out; throughout the action she taps pathetically on the kitchen window, soaked to the skin. Sidney ignores her until the guests have left (prematurely) and he is able to declare the evening a success. Ever submissive to her bossy, ambitious husband, Jane dries herself, empties her wellies and, stifling tears, ends the act happily consoled in her favourite activity, cleaning the floor.

This first act is perfect comic artifice; the farce arises out of situation, which in turn is caused by character. The language is very precisely observed; the social layers revealed in the way each man talks to or about his partner: Sidney refers to 'the wife' instead of 'my wife', philanderer Geoffrey ingratiates with 'Eva – darling', whilst Ronald refers to his more than capable wife as 'old girl'. The women are similarly well drawn in relationship to their men. Marion controls both her husband and her sometime lover with suave upper-middle-class social confidence; Eva struggles for self control, and control of her husband's appetites, like a cornered cat. Jane, always the anxious subservient slave, agrees with everybody.

The scene is set for two more hysterically funny Christmases. The first in Eva's filthy untidy kitchen where Christmas has been completely forgotten as Geoffrey struggles to run a marriage, an affair and a disintegrating career and Eva is driven in desperation towards suicide. Not that Geoffrey notices; he is much too concerned with organizing the dismantling of his marriage. 'Believe me darling, you were right... And it's absolutely true that the best thing that could happen to you and me, at this point in our lives, is for me to go and live with Sally.'

The hurriedly arranged party is turned to comic disarray because not one of the guests who strays into the kitchen notices that poor Eva is trying in various ways to kill herself. Marion, leisured but ignored gentlewoman, is floating on an excess of gin; Ronald is bumbling his way through repairing a broken light-fitting. Sidney, now more at ease in these circles, is organizing everyone and repairing a blocked sink drain. Jane is, of course, happily cleaning the oven and mopping the floor. By the end of the act, however, the scene is one of total disarray. Sidney is covered in the oven grease from Jane's bucket, Ronald has been electrocuted and sits under a therapeutic layer of newly washed underwear and tea towels, and Marion is practically unconscious with alcohol. Eva leads them all, a desperately unhappy and flattened group, in a chorus of 'The Twelve Days of Christmas'.

It is a complete picture of disintegration. All dignity is denied anyone who arrived at the party with it. However, once again, because of the personalities of those involved, it is a very funny image.

When we reach Act 3, we can see that it is also a metaphor for the disintegration of the social order. For in it we are shown

21

Marion and Ronald's kitchen. She is now an alcoholic, retreating, almost permanently, upstairs to bed, and he is shivering downstairs unable to get the central heating to work. He has never understood women, he says: 'One minute you're having a perfectly good time and the next, you suddenly see them there like – some old sports jacket or something – literally coming apart at the seams'.

Their visitors are equally troubled. Geoffrey has lost his mistress and most of his professional reputation. Eva, newly recovered from her depression, is trying to get his career and her marriage back in order with the grim, mirthless, determination of the desperate. It is not much of a Christmas celebration.

But Santa arrives – in the unwelcome form of Sidney Hopcroft – and, though they try at first to hide, they cannot escape him. He is now a very successful property tycoon, and he treats the assembled company with the largess of the powerful. He is able to rib Geoffrey for his latest architectural disaster and to bully Ronald with offers of potential business favours. He is a very happy, contented boor, dispensing inappropriate presents and funny disguises. The final image of the play is a macabre comic dance orchestrated by the Hopcrofts. The bank manager and his wife, the architect and his earnest partner, are put through humiliating forfeits as Sydney controls the music and commands them to 'Dance...Come on...Dance!'

Absurd Person Singular is as cruel as it is laughable. For, as it moves across its three acts, it traces the disintegration of a comfortable social order and its transformation into a merit-ocracy. Here values are less certain, and the bully and the venal can triumph. The end of ambition is success and it is also power. Alan Ayckbourn always fears and mistrusts power because its abuse creates and exploits the underdog. At the close of this play, we see many forms of power – sexual, social and professional – grabbed by Sidney Hopcroft as he dictates the action, blackmails for sexual favours, and displays the fruits of his success.

The whole action of this remarkable play is a picture too of a more general truth; the disintegration, change and decay that underline the human condition. As Benedict Nightingale puts it, 'Like everything else in Ayckbourn's bleak, funny world, time itself is deeply inimical to hope, effort, fulfilment and happiness'. It is the loss of all these elements that *Absurd Person Singular* explores through its glimpse behind the festive façade to the offstage action.

The Norman Conquests (1973) is a trilogy of plays, perhaps most famous for having no offstage action. By making the offstage action of one play the onstage action of another, the whole work describes an eventful weekend in a house. Each play stands alone, but each contains the offstage action unseen but implied in the other two. When a character moves from one room in the first play, he enters another setting in the next one. Thus, to see all three plays is to see all the action both onstage and off. It is an incredible demonstration of playwriting skill, which enhances immeasurably the performances for those audience members who see more than one of the three plays.

But it is not just the technical feat that sticks in the mind on seeing these plays. As Frank Rich says, '*The Norman Conquests* is not only funny but impossibly wise about sex, marriage, love and loneliness'. Alan Ayckbourn turns once more to focus on the sexual and social mores which govern the interplay of men and women.

In Ayckbourn's plays the family home is the crucible in which the concept of the family can be tested. When a family get together to celebrate or to holiday, the intention is probably as Norman declares: 'For god's sake, this is family...if we don't care, brothers, sisters, husbands, wives...If we can't finally join hands, what hope is there for anybody?' It clearly strikes a chord with everyone on stage and probably those in the auditorium. The problem is that the getting together of a family group often accentuates all the stresses in family life. Individual people are sometimes strained to breaking point at a celebratory event. Alan Ayckbourn constantly makes merry with this irony of the human condition turning the observation of its consequences into social comment.

In scenes such as the dinner party in *Table Manners*, the first of the trilogy, the family rituals that the organizer, Sarah, thinks will bind them together become the cause of aggravation. Just seating people leads to squabbling, and try as she might she cannot get people to sit exactly where she wants them. One poor soul ends up on an impossibly low stool, another couple exchange insults until blows are struck; small talk turns into big rows.

Like many others throughout Alan Ayckbourn's work, the family in *The Norman Conquests* is not a benign structure. It is presided over by a character whom we never see; the matriarch of this household lies bedridden upstairs. But her presence pervades the action. Her children recount horror stories of her sexual past. Immoral, selfish and oversexed, she seems to have blighted her children with her self-obsession and bullying.

One daughter, Annie the eternal spinster carer, is chained to the duty of looking after her. She seeks a loving relationship with Tom, a local vet who is impossibly dim and indecisive. He will probably never get round to asking her to marry him and she seems doomed to always have to 'pot Mother, and retire to bed – alone – itching'. Her brother, Reg, seems so scourged by his upbringing that he has retired into an extended adolescence of hobbies, making models and inventing complicated board games. No wonder his obsessive, orderly wife, Sarah, is bossy to the point of exasperation. The other daughter, Ruth, has found escape in being a careerist, and married librarian Norman, more or less because she can treat him as a pet. 'It's a bit like owning an oversized unmanageable dog', she says. 'He's not very well house-trained, he needs continual exercising...and it's sensible to lock him up if you have any visitors.'

Norman is the catalyst within this motley band of characters. More precisely, it is his thirst for sex and for adulation which upsets the family equilibrium. 'He never makes a gesture unless there is an appreciate audience to applaud him.' And he cannot resist the gauntlet thrown down by henpecked Reg when he asserts that a marriage might be reinvigorated were husband or wife to go off with someone else for a few days. Not, Reg adds, that this applies to his wife. 'Sarah would never dream of going off.'

Norman sets about this challenge, not only pursuing Sarah but playing each of the three women off one against the other; declaring to each, 'I'd like to see you happy...I'd very much like to make you happy'. Of course, what Norman really wants is to make himself happy, since this is his only real purpose in life. He is perhaps a male counterpart to the unseen dominant figure upstairs in bed.

And these women are very ready for his sexual invitation, for each one has a desperate loneliness at the heart of her own relationships. Because he acts the part that each one wants him

24

to play, they see his advances as an escape into personal fulfilment. But it is a fleeting happiness. If, in Ayckbourn's plays, the collapse of marriage is the collapse of fantasy, it can never be replaced by the retreat into another delusion. The weekend is a miserable disaster for everyone except Norman. He has spent the night with Ruth, anticipates his promised dirty weekend with Annie, and Sarah is hovering on the point of sexual cooperation. Ruthlessly, he stage-manages a car crash in the drive so that everyone must stay for another night. The image of Annie's cat being coaxed down to earth from the tree comes into focus. Perhaps Sarah too will be coaxed out of her lofty safety net, now that the opportunity has been engineered.

Norman is like many of Ayckbourn's central male characters. Their role is to be the cause of chaos, infecting and upsetting the status quo. Sometimes, like Norman, they are too self obsessed to notice, and sometimes they are painfully aware of the effect they are having, but quite unable to handle the situation.

In *Season's Greetings* (1980), for instance, our hero is a shy author invited to spend Christmas with a family gathering by a spinster bookworm. His very presence arouses sexual desire in the women of the household as each seeks solace from their indifferent or disappointing partner. In one night he is attacked on the stairs by the evasive virgin advances of Rachel, and astonished to receive a proposition from the family drunk. He is dragged with unbridled passion by his hostess, Pattie, from room to room before finally having his clothes torn off under the Christmas tree. This indiscretion is witnessed by the whole household assembled on the stairs, summoned by the drumming of a mechanical toy. Our hero and his hostess are discovered frantically tearing open Christmas wrapping to find and silence it. Ayckbourn's men are frequently embarrassed or defeated by toys and inanimate objects.

Their problem is, most often, that they feel themselves to be in charge but cannot always cope. Social convention insists that they are the head of the household and yet, try as they might, they seem doomed to be defeated by the bewildering complexity of their lives. Sometimes they retreat into useless hobbies, as Bernard does in *Season's Greetings* with his puppet show. But, as usual, it is another object waiting to trap him. His show – surely one of the most hilarious play-within-a-play scenes in all comedy – ends as a humiliating fiasco.

25

Yet still these husbands are driven by hubris to undertake mannish tasks such as repairing clocks or lawnmowers. In *Just Between Ourselves* (1976) Dennis is almost permanently in his garage fiddling with household repairs. However, the results seem to be rather disappointing and, in the case of at least one kettle, downright dangerous. But there he is safe from the two women in his home, who fight over the right to play out the traditional female role of carer for the man of the house. Both wife and mother turn to him (presumably as nominal head of the household) to intervene in their petty jealous disputes. This he is singularly unfit to do, just as he is incapable of fixing the garage door to remove the car he wants to sell. His potential purchaser is Neil, who finds it equally difficult to act the role of ruthless bargain hunter, to the evident contempt of his wife, Pam. The two men, both inadequate to the role of master in their own homes, strike up a friendship based on their escape into Dennis's world of inconsequential do-it-yourself.

The catastrophe is that what really needs repair is Dennis's marriage. Vera his wife has suffered what Dennis euphemistically calls 'what shall I say...a few health worries'. Not surprising really, considering her mother-in-law's constant carping as they both vie for the affections of the man in the home. When Vera pathetically asks for help, Dennis with his total incapacity to tackle anything difficult says 'Yes, well I tell you what. When you've got a moment, why don't you sit down, get a bit of paper and just make a little list of all the things you would like me to help you with. Things you'd like me to do, things that need mending or fixing, and then we can talk about them.' It is a crushingly cruel moment, but typical of Ayckbourn's men and the havoc that they wreak on their women.

Dennis is not deliberately cruel to Vera; he is incapable of coping. Like many men in Ayckbourn's world, he is indecisive, postponing decisions because he feels inadequate to the circumstances or a victim of conflicting loyalties. His way of tackling Vera's problem is to make her the butt of jokes or to patronize her. She fights to maintain her sanity, but it is not easy. At the birthday party given for Dennis, everyone watches nervously as she serves tea with violently shaking hands. They are all aware of the knife edge her sanity is on but unable to tackle it properly because of suburban politeness, or inadequate interpersonal skills. Dennis can barely stifle giggles of embarrassment; with thumping callousness he sings an ironic 'Happy Birthday to me'. It is small wonder that, by the end of the play, we discover Vera sitting in the garden wrapped in a rug to protect her against the chill of the wind. She has lost her battle to maintain her sanity and sits motionless in a catatonic state.

So many women in Alan Ayckbourn's plays fight a losing battle against their marital circumstances. They struggle to maintain dignity within their relationships, but it is a hard conflict. Torn between duty and personal happiness, they suffer embarrassment, neglect and even cruelty. Roles are clearly defined in this world: men do not lay tables, look after children, prepare food. Women, saddled with these functions, tend to treat their men as children or pets. And they seem doomed to suffer disappointment and lack of fulfilment. Small wonder that they frequently reach breaking point.

In *Absent Friends* (1974) Diana actually breaks down onstage, gibbering something about always wanting to be a Mountie. But 'little girls don't join the mounted police. Little girls do nice things like typing, knitting and nursing and having babies. So I married Paul instead.' She too has suffered humiliation by her partner at a gathering designed to console a bereaved friend. But friends, as this much underrated play insists, are hard to define, and are bonded by their own definitions of friendship, not a legal contract. Though nominally a caring assembly, these six people are isolated by their individual self-interest. As their sexual, social or professional drives dictate, their loyalties and their definitions of friendship shift. It is their bereaved one-time friend Colin who brings this to a comic climax. When he refuses to be a desolate mourner, he is blissfully unaware that he might aggravate relationships that have a history of which he knows nothing. A cheerful idealist (a personality Ayckbourn mistrusts in the way Ibsen did), he has only gleefully sunny memories. But this group of friends have moved on and his picture of friendship past is a catastrophic catalyst when it activates division and breakdown. For what Colin sees as strengths in their marriages, they recognize as the real weaknesses. Above all he has not recognized the power struggles and the consequent roles of victim and abuser at the heart of their marriages.

Surely, one might ask, there are some successful happy couples around? Some friendships that are not blighted by self-interest? Are there no Beautiful People? Ayckbourn says: 'I think that's where the tensions come nowadays...in leading us to expect beautiful people. There are about twenty five beautiful people.' And he does show us at least three of them in *Joking Apart* (1978). Richard and Anthea are two of the nicest people that could ever invite you to be their friend, and their daughter Debbie will grow to be the same. Beautiful, kind, generous and successful, they host a series of ritual festivities: bonfire night, Christmas, garden party and birthday disco, and their friends come along. There is Sven – a self-important Finn who is a business partner to Richard – with his wife Olive. Their next door neighbour Hugh, the newly installed vicar, brings Louise his wife and their brat child. And there is Brian, a one-time boyfriend of Anthea, still holding an unfulfilled love for her but accompanied by a series of eminently unsuitable girlfriends.

All these girls look surprisingly familiar, which is hardly surprising since Ayckbourn insists that they are all played by the actress who finally plays Debbie, the ideal daughter. This simple theatrical device reinforces the notion that Brian is desperately seeking to replace the golden Anthea. But as outsiders, they can see what those within the enchanted circle of friendship cannot. Richard and Anthea's overwhelming generosity – food, drinks, kindnesses and understanding – has a stifling effect on them all. Self-important Sven, who 'nods approvingly at nature as he walks', puts it succinctly. 'As friends, be careful of them...No, I'll say nothing more. Be Careful.' He has already felt the cold wind within this friendship. Richard is much the most successful business partner even though, naturally gifted, he need put in half the effort; Sven feels himself undermined but denied just cause for complaint. Brian is caught in an emotional trap that he will never escape. We see him get older and less desirable as he clings to his unrequited love for Anthea over the fourteen year timescale of the play. The vicar next door, Hugh, shortly after he has moved in, sees the fence between their vicarage and Richard's house torn down so both families can share a larger communal garden. Soon he too is embroiled in unfulfilled desire for Anthea, and his own wife subsides through jealousy into desperation and finally a nervous breakdown.

This is all caused not by spite, nor ambition, nor heartlessness. What Ayckbourn paints is a picture of what Michael Billington calls 'the blithe destructiveness of the good'. In the unfair distribution of good luck there are many victims; at the end of this play, we see a gang of losers. They are a pathetic bunch: crippled by heart attacks, pathetically clinging to their lost youth, sedated with Valium. Richard and Anthea who, significantly, have never formalized their relationship into a legal marriage, gather waifs around them to cherish: perhaps the motive is power, as Sven suggests. But it may truly be kindness; and the effect that other people's good fortune has of reinforcing one's own feelings of inadequacy may be an unfortunate by-product of charity.

It is an exploration of man's unconscious inhumanity to man that forms the heart of Alan Ayckbourn's work. Audiences rock with laughter at these plays; they contain many wonderful scenes of comic dialogue and farcical action. But at their heart is a disenchantment born out of this playwright's affinity with the underdog. He sees underdogs everywhere, amongst men and women, in families and friendships, sympathetic personalities and unsympathetic ones. As he says to Ian Watson, 'My biggest recurrent theme is that people do care about each other; it's just that they handle each other in boxing gloves most of the time... And I remember that all the screaming and shouting and hurling of food against the walls that happened in my early relationship had to do with wanting to get closer to that person I wanted to share my life with. It wasn't that I wanted to hurt them (although occasionally I did because I felt they were hurting me). It was to do with caring and loving: it wasn't to do with anything destructive.'

3

Technical Directions

By *Season's Greetings* (1980), Alan Ayckbourn had a proven track record of West End success and an international reputation as a comic playwright. This and the plays that followed show a total command of technical and comedic resources. This chapter will survey some of them to analyse and demonstrate his craftsmanship.

Ayckbourn was by now regarded as capable of making a popular audience laugh whilst exploring his subjects with a kindly objectivity that could cast a dark shadow over the laughter. He was frequently compared to Neil Simon, the equally successful American comic dramatist. But it has often been pointed out that, though they are both theatrical craftsmen of great skill, they work in quite different ways.

Simon is the master of the one-liner joke; Ayckbourn tries to edit out such jokes. Laughter in the English writer's plays comes from what characters do because of who they are and because they are at the mercy of each other, and of circumstance. They cannot construct careful barbed verbal responses for self-protection as Neil Simon's characters can. Simon's background is as a scriptwriter primarily focused on words; Ayckbourn's is as a director, and he relishes working with visual action and actors.

Alan Ayckbourn has always insisted that he is as much a theatre director as he is a playwright. He has been artistic director of the Stephen Joseph Theatre in Scarborough since 1970, with responsibility for directing the majority of plays mounted in any one season and for writing at least one play a year which will keep the organization solvent. It is this dual role that informs his plays and strengthens them technically. It has given him the opportunity to experiment to a quite remarkable degree. The plays written for the company question the

Aristotelian unities of time and place with a mounting disregard for precedent. They become increasingly fluid in both location and time, shifting within both, and challenging the authority of the playwright to dictate narrative structure.

Ayckbourn is given less than due credit for these experiments for two reasons: subject matter and milieu remain largely within a particular set of parameters, and they are underpinned by a secure dramatic technique which arises out of his directing experience and consequently never undermines the actor. An experiment is never an end in itself but always a means to secure an appropriate framework for the exploration of a theme. Though he may create an elaborate multiple setting, as in *Taking Steps* (1979), he is more interested in the story – of frustrated hope and ambitions for instance – than in the scenic device. The actor's prime purpose – to demonstrate the human condition – is never undermined, no matter how innovative the dramatic framework. Performers quickly recognize the security of superb technical expertise in the play writing.

It is essential to analyse some of that craft and to explore its roots. Ayckbourn is a master of plot construction, a wordsmith of great precision and an organizer of moments placed in the action to comic perfection. But he is also more fully aware of the theatre's technical equipment and its possibilities than any other dramatist, and he sees the limitations of a stage as a challenge and a source of inspiration. A glance at one or two plays demonstrates this.

As we have already seen, all the plays are impeccably plotted and shaped, exploiting their two-act structure with carefully placed comic and dramatic climaxes. Starting with his theme, Ayckbourn will spend many months organizing the structure before he ever tackles dialogue; the scripts are thus often written in a few days, but as a result of a very long planning period. He has already identified protagonists on both sides of his theme's argument and frequently another character 'to provide the motor to the action'. Thus his plays are strong architectural constructions within which actor and director can develop the action. But sound plotting is only the start of his skills.

There is also in all Ayckbourn a great precision in the use of language. Two examples from *Taking Steps* illustrate the sensitivity to speech patterns and the care with which words

31

are placed. Shy Tristram, a newly qualified solicitor, has arrived in place of his boss Mr Winthrop to present papers for signing. He explains to Mr Boxer:

'Yes...Sorry, my name's...No, I'm from Speake, Tacket and... er...Whatsname...Sorry. Hot. I'm – my name's...er ...well, I'm here on behalf of Mr. Winthrop who's been...er... taken ill, you see. Not seriously. So, I'm here instead.'

The whole speech is a wonderful character sketch of a very anxious young man labouring under his first responsibility. But the word 'Hot' seems at first either misplaced or a non sequitur, until one realizes that it is an excuse to cover embarrassment. Then it seems perfectly positioned to give the actor maximum opportunity, especially when, almost immediately, it is followed by the confusing double meaning of 'Not seriously'.

Equally well placed is the final word in a speech from pompous bucket manufacturer Roland Crabbe, who, suspecting poor shy Tristram of having slept with his wife, takes him out into the corridor and quietly menaces him with this threat: 'And make no mistake, I have influence. Not in all quarters maybe but many. Let's just say, I could make life very difficult for you if you ever wanted to get into hardware.' The ludicrous final word deflates the threat and punctures Roland's pomposity to hilarious effect.

As in all great comic writing, characters show us what they are by what they do and say. But they rarely explain themselves to us. Self-justifying explanations, when they do occur, are often careless remarks, inadvertently revealing more than characters would want us to know. Indeed, careless slips of the tongue are frequently the windows through which we see the true depths of despair and loneliness that hide behind carefully crafted façades. In *Woman in Mind* (1985) Susan is told that her son, who has joined a sect and not been in contact for two years, is coming home. But it is only to clear his old room of the furniture he left behind in order to sell it. She blurts out, 'But...That's all that's left of him...If we sell...his bed...and his swivel chair...then we'll have nothing left of him at all...I won't be able to sit in there, now. Like I do.' A few unguarded words and we glimpse a picture of a profoundly lonely woman, sitting in her son's empty room, seeking comfort. These accidental revelations are to be found throughout Ayckbourn's plays.

Often ignored technical skills are never abandoned by Ayckbourn. For example, characters in an Ayckbourn play are never left without a covering line for entrance or exit. An appropriate remark, usually of explanation or justification, is always there to motivate and cover the move. But this technical necessity in Ayckbourn's skilful hands becomes an opportunity for a further fleshing out of character or plot.

For instance, in *Sisterly Feelings* (1979) Stafford comes stamping up the slope:

DORCAS: Are they coming?
STAFFORD: Stupid old bag has fallen down a hole.
ABIGAIL: Who has?
DORCAS: Rita. She's OK.
STAFFORD: My shoes are leaking.
DORCAS: Good, it'll wash your feet. Did you push her?
STAFFORD: Who?
DORCAS: Auntie Rita.
STAFFORD: No, her fascist husband wasn't it?

So, Ayckbourn gives Stafford a great line to enter with, which is picked up by others onstage and which promotes more character-led comedy invective. Dorcas's enquiry, which in the hands of a lesser dramatist would alone have served to cover the entrance, is never answered. But it ignites dialogue telling us more about the personalities onstage and what they feel about each other. Stafford on the other hand is given more motivation to colour his arrival with an inconsequential problem that diverts his focus from the conversation and allows the entrance to culminate in a vivid insult joke.

At the opening of most of his plays, Ayckbourn contrives a starter motor for the comedy. A well honed set-piece joke provokes the audience to initial laughter. This is from *Ten Times Table* (1977), set in the ballroom of the Swan Hotel:

In the semi-darkness, Ray, an enthusiastic man in his forties, enters...

RAY (*to someone off behind him*): Right, thank you (*He turns*) Hoy! Hoy – I say. There's no light in here. Could we have some lights on in here, please? Lights. Yes. Lights... (*clicking of switches*) No... No... No...
(*The lights go on*)
That's it.
(*The lights go off*)

No. The last one you did. No. The one before that.
(*The lights go on*)
That's it. Thank you. Fine.

The opportunities for director and actor are obvious; a simple comic situation inviting acting and directing skill to kick start the audience into laughter. As Michael Billington points out, Alan Ayckbourn is primarily a visual playwright. He understands the primacy of dramatic narrative which is a narrative of action – not of words. What is funny is most often what the audience sees as much as what it hears. His scripts are skilful constructions of both elements; to read only the ill timed or thoughtless remark, without visualizing the ironic consequences for all participants onstage, is to ignore the real strength of a playwright who is also one of his generation's most experienced theatre directors. This playwright has an encyclopaedic knowledge of the technical resources of the theatre and knows how to deploy all of them for his narrative. In this respect he is again like the film 'auteur'.

One sequence in *Bedroom Farce* (1975) demonstrates Ayckbourn's mastery of lighting effects and his understanding of their possibilities. The stage picture is of three rooms set side by side. We see the yuppie bedroom of Nick and Jan's flat and that of Malcolm and Kate in their newly acquired brick terrace house, simultaneously with Ernest and Delia's comfortable bedroom in their large Victorian pile. The domestic harmony in each one is shattered by visits from the neurotic Susannah and the selfish Trevor, who bring their post-divorce angst to disrupt their friends' sleeping hours.

As the action switches from room to room, the focus is drawn by lighting states, a common enough device. But in one sequence, the lights are merely raised in each room in turn in a sort of résumé of the plot so far. Susannah has decided to stay overnight, sharing Delia's bed, and Trevor has similarly disrupted the sleep of the other households. We see middle-aged Delia having to suffer Susannah moaning neurotically in her sleep. 'Oh Lord', Delia sighs as the light fades on her. It rises next on Kate in bed alone under the bedclothes whilst her husband Malcolm, surprisingly, lies on the floor. He has fallen asleep sandpapering the floorboards. The light then cross-fades to Jan trapped under her prostrate husband who cannot move having slipped a disc. He wails an apology and she resigns

34

herself to a sleepless night. A moment later we are drawn by the lighting back to Delia and her moaning bed mate. It is a *coup de théâtre* occasioned with a minimum of dialogue by Ayckbourn's understanding of the comic pictures he has contrived and the potential of elementary theatre technology. The lighting states replace action to create the laughter. It is impossible to think of any other playwright who uses modern technical facilities to such comic narrative effect.

With his own theatre to experiment in, it is little wonder that Ayckbourn demonstrates such adroit technical skill. In fact, the tiny stage at Westwood, which the Ayckbourn company built from an old school hall and used between 1976 and 1996, was a very specific and, some might conclude, restrictive space. The stage was a twenty-foot square with a wide entrance on one side and two narrow ones on the opposite corners. The 250 seats rose up steeply in blocks all around the acting area. The lighting grid was fifteen feet from the stage floor and almost within reach of audience members on the back rows.

It sounds an unpromising space but its geography seems to have been a challenge to Ayckbourn to push the possibilities for its use to the limits. The result has been some remarkable and innovative uses of space and of location. The action of his plays has been set on canal boats surrounded by real water (*Way Upstream*, 1981), on golf courses (*Intimate Exchanges*, 1982), in swimming pools (*Man of the Moment*, 1988), and frequently a multiplicity of venues within one play (*The Revengers' Comedies*, 1989; *Intimate Exchanges*, 1982; *Taking Steps*, 1979).

Taking Steps accepts the challenges of a restricted stage area and turns it to advantage. It is worth taking time to examine this play in detail; it demonstrates many of Ayckbourn's technical skills and his use of them to support both plot and thematic structures. It contains some hilarious verbal jokes which are carefully planted in one act and capitalized on in the next, some used three times over to increasing effect. There are comic characters too, and moments engineered to maximum effect. But it is Ayckbourn's use of the stage space that is most astounding. The audience is confronted with a setting unlike any other, in which spatial geometry has disintegrated. The irony is that this scenic device is there to enhance the farce and to reflect more perfectly the dramatist's purpose. Theme and spatial experiment are intertwined.

35

Elizabeth, a frustrated dancer with a very melodramatic personality, is leaving her husband, Roland. She has written her farewell note, a perfect example of Ayckbourn's wordplay, and asks her brother, Mark, to read it out loud.

> My darling, maybe this letter will not come as that much of a surprise to you after all. Quite simply by the time you read this, I will be gone. As you once said of me, and it is a moment I will always treasure, my darling, I am a woman who needs an endless amount of – something – feeling. An endless amount of feeling. Farming. Fencing. Fancying. Ferrets? . . .

The word Mark is searching for turns out to be 'freedom'. This verbal joke is the comic starting motor and the play's theme in microcosm – the struggle for personal liberation, a desire frequently misunderstood or misinterpreted and most often resented. Ayckbourn is expanding a recurring motif – the necessity to resist the expectations of others. Elizabeth is trying to break loose from a life planned and run by her man, and to find self-expression through a career as a dancer. The letter is a rather cowardly way of avoiding the overbearing manner of her husband, Roland Crabbe. Its misinterpretation as a suicide note is the mainspring of the farce's action.

Mark's fiancée, Kitty, has been arrested, apparently for soliciting on Haverstock Hill, which sounds like another misunderstanding since she is rather timid and finds it very difficult to assert herself. But she too has decided to be free of her fiancé, who is so boring that he sends a number of people in the play to sleep (literally) with his conversation. Both Elizabeth and Kitty believe that they are trapped and can find happiness only by breaking free from their partners' control. They are different, however, as Ayckbourn points out: 'Kitty may escape because she is prepared to chance everything to achieve it, Elizabeth would still like to take a small slice of cake with her to eat later'. No wonder. Her husband, Roland, is a very successful businessman. He provides well for his beloved Lizzie. But he also bullies and domineers everyone including an oily landlord and an exceptionally gauche solicitor who have come to conclude Crabbe's purchase of the house.

This young solicitor is the personification of innocence. Tristram Watson speaks in a manner so tongue-tied that no one can penetrate it. His shy manner marks him as an obvious candidate for manipulation by more forceful personalities. And sure enough, he spends the action of the play being pushed around the house by everybody, from one farcical situation to another. If the women are under the thumbs of their men, Tristram is bullied by everyone – husband, fiancée, wife, builder.

He presents a comic counterpoint to the two women and their plans to escape unhappy stifling relationships. For, paradoxically, he is manoeuvred into situations which offer him potential happiness and even sexual bliss. He finds Kitty locked in the attic airing cupboard, and in releasing her discovers a soul mate. They stumble and stutter a recognition of shared experience. We suspect that the relationship which is initiated here between two of life's underdogs might provide both of them with freedom from the domineering natures of others. Perhaps Ayckbourn offers us, for once, the idea that the innocent and the meek may find just reward.

But not before Tristram has slept with Roland Crabbe's wife! The house it seems was once a brothel and is reputedly haunted by the ghost of one of the girls who was murdered there. She, 'Scarlet Lucy', is said to appear occasionally and to revenge herself by sleeping with men; the catch is that they never wake up again. Elizabeth, having second thoughts about leaving, returns to a dark house and slips into bed alongside what she supposes is her husband. It is, however, a wide-eyed and terrified Tristram. When he wakes next morning, terror transforms into rhapsody over his lost virginity; he says, 'Dear God, thank you for a wonderful, wonderful night'. This is the first line of Act 2 and is another piece of immaculate comic engineering.

But what really transforms the action is the setting. *Taking Steps* plays one of Ayckbourn's most intriguing spatial jokes. It is set in The Pines, an old Victorian house which rambles through three floors. It has an attic on top, a bedroom level and a ground floor with living room and kitchen. The twist is that we see everything at once, superimposed on one flat stage. The staircases are horizontal, with steps up indicated by stair rods laid in a flat carpet. Ayckbourn is able to present action on all three floors simultaneously in one plane. The sofa in the living room downstairs is only inches away from the bed on the first floor, which in turn is feet away from the airing cupboard in the attic. The farcical possibilities are exploited to the full.

The audience soon realizes that, though Lizzie may walk within inches of Tristram, she is on the second floor and he is sitting downstairs unaware that she is in the house. No wonder his face reveals that he is half persuaded the place might truly be haunted. At one point, Lizzie practises a balletic leap from her bed, landing between two people who are one floor below her. Plaster from the living room ceiling falls, of course, on the heads of the two outer figures.

This is a daring and unique spatial experiment, sustained by Ayckbourn's consummate technical ease. It is beautifully integrated into plot and serves the dramatist's theme perfectly. These characters may inhabit the same space but they are too self-obsessed to be consistently aware of each other's desires, of each other's reality.

What Ayckbourn is also able to achieve with this scenic convention is a cinematic effect. We can roam about the house, cutting from floor to floor, room to room, without the actor having to leave the stage, or any scene change. The audience acts as camera and editor, switching shot from upstairs to down instantly. By capitalizing on the limitations of a restrictive stage area, Ayckbourn turns it to his advantage and invites the audience into the process of editing the images.

Alan Ayckbourn's employing filmic conventions should not surprise us. His love of cinema and its methods has influenced his output greatly, as we shall see. When questioned recently about his technical skills, his answer was interesting. The reason why we have so much 'director's theatre', he claims, is because the young playwright hands over so much to the realizer. Technique for Ayckbourn is a means of control over the realization of his script. But it is not control for its own sake. It is a skilful weaving of means of delivery and theme together. The action is manifest onstage in the way most appropriate to the theme, even if that means employing technical facilities and equipment in unconventional ways. Sometimes it means breaking accepted rules of theatrical method. It is essentially the writer for the stage becoming 'auteur' – a term more usually associated with the film creator and implying the fusing of script and image under the control of the prime film-maker, the director.

That Ayckbourn sees his role as akin to that of a cinematic

auteur is underlined in his 1996 televised lecture at the University of Wales in Cardiff. He said: 'People ask what were my stage influences... my stage influences were almost entirely from cinema. I spent the whole of my misspent youth in cinema. My stage geography [sic] is in fact, I suppose, the sort of grammar that is common in film rather than on stage. I use the cut, the superimposed shot and so on which are more or less clichés in the film these days but still novel and unusual in the theatre. It means that action can be moved very quickly... Narrative techniques have speeded up... thanks to Film and TV... Film techniques have a vital part to play in the staging of my plays today'.

His ambition for the vitality of a filmic, seamless narrative is shared by many modern dramatists, but few have the technical knowledge and the expertise to achieve it. That Ayckbourn does can be seen in the two plays which form *The Revengers' Comedies* (1989).

The action switches continually between many locations, starting with a suicide attempt on Albert Bridge in London, roaming around various rooms of Furtherfield House and the offices of mega business Lembridge Tennit, and out into the fields of Anthony Staxton-Billing's farm. A glimpse at the scene list in the published script shows no fewer than twenty different locations specified. Even more remarkably, each one is given a time to the nearest quarter of an hour when the action takes place. The author is thinking about lighting states even as he is constructing the action.

It is a technically demanding concept, more like a film montage than a theatre piece. Ayckbourn's original production in Scarborough moved with consummate ease, using only essential furniture or scenic elements. It enabled him to present us with a theatre version of a British film comedy. The cast list reads as a gallery of eccentric characters drawn from an outdated social structure: Percy Cutting, Tracey Willingforth, Imogen Staxton-Billing, Councillor Daphne Teale, Bruce Tick. It is a seductively recognizable comic milieu, with characters defined by their evocative names, drawing us into the Will Hayes/Ealing tradition. The plot has equally familiar movie antecedents, instantly recognizable as a reworking of Hitchcock's *Strangers on a Train*.

However, this is a cozy trap to lure us towards the second play, which completes the action. For here the comedy assumes grotesque proportions; Henry Bell's pact with Karen Knightly for the solving of each other's problems turns from dream solution into nightmare driven by fanaticism. Ms Knightly is revealed as distinctly unbalanced, ruthless and obsessive in her determination to eliminate enemies, real and imagined. One cannot but be tempted to see political allegory in this play written at the end of the Thatcher premiership. The lady crusades through the offices of Lembridge Tennit with unbending zeal. In Ayckbourn's original Scarborough production she strode down corridors of light, in and out of lifts created by sound and lighting effects, holding telephone conversations picked out in individual spotlights with a distant Henry Bell. The stage directions are distinctly filmic and have a double effect. Firstly, they underline Karen's insane tunnel vision as the lighting isolates her. At the same time, they enlarge the visual statement. The effects, technically simple enough, enable Ayckbourn to suggest that the office block is a corporate warren and that we can encompass this, and indeed the whole of Karen's world, by cutting or cross-fading in the way a film editor might. We are given the freedom to visit almost any part of her domain and it reinforces the notion that this Ealing comedy has a larger purpose and vision.

But Ayckbourn will always shy away from too easy a political reference; it is not his real purpose. He is using the Ealing tradition of comic caricature and familiar locations in exaggerated form to make a more universal statement. For Karen, winning every difficult situation is no problem; you simply play by rules of your own making. It is a ruthless philosophy but a winning one. 'Life is not a game', says Henry Bell, 'There's a much bigger board, for one thing. People keep stealing your counters and changing the rules. Life's a lot more complicated and a good deal harder to play.' Indeed it is, and as Kalson has pointed out, Ayckbourn is at pains to remind us that goodness is not enough. Power, whether it be in corporate or petty local government form, will be for ever in the hands of the few at the top of the pile. 'Easy-Peasy', says the immoral Ms Knightly. People like her will always rule the game board. When Karen throws herself off the Albert Bridge at the end of the play, Henry

Bell is set free to settle into a loving marriage with Imogen Staxton-Billing. However, Ayckbourn implies that he will continue to be one of those innocents who will always suffer at the fanatic whim of life's power players. Some people play life for the pleasure of the game, but they will always be at the mercy of those who play to win.

A further example of Ayckbourn's technical skills and his adoption of filmic conventions is to be seen by examining the opening stage directions to *Woman in Mind* (1985).

'Darkness' is the first stage direction, a common enough theatrical starting point but one which here assumes a dramatic purpose. For out of it dawns a picture of the vicarage garden with Susan, the vicar's wife, prostrate on the ground tended by her friend Dr Bill Windsor (one of a whole gallery of incompetent medics who inhabit this playwright's work). Susan has been concussed after stepping on the end of a garden rake. The first few minutes of dialogue are a mixture of gibberish from Bill – 'Wo! Won't spider slit up pikelet' – and distressed incomprehension from Susan– 'Why have I gone to hell? Why me? I've tried so terribly hard, too. Terribly hard'. Suddenly she understands what Bill is saying, as he identifies her by name. 'Susan, yes thank heavens', she answers in relief. But Ayckbourn has his opening big joke ready: 'December bee?' says Bill. 'December bee. Oh dear god, he's off again', Susan cries.

The stage directions offer explanation: *'Throughout the play we will hear what she hears, see what she sees. A subjective viewpoint therefore and one that may at times be somewhat less than accurate.'* The lighting effect and dialogue imitate her regaining consciousness and the dawning recognition of her familiar surroundings. With minimum effort the convention is clear; by using action and the simplest of technical means, Ayckbourn has explained to the audience the comment he has hidden in the stage directions.

Another stage direction tells us that Susan is *'an unassuming woman in her forties, used to and happy to play second fiddle to more determined personalities than her own'*. But the audience, awakening with Susan, must wait to have this one elucidated. For when her family first emerges, they are a most engaging group, healthy, charming and totally dedicated, offering champagne, love and consideration. Pleasing Susan seems the object of their existence.

41

They are, of course figments of her imagination, the result of her accident and general state of mind. Consequently, they are overwhelmingly ideal and a disturbing contrast to the untidy, bumblingly incompetent, and all too real figure of her friend Dr Bill Windsor.

After ten minutes of the play, Susan and the audience are in the same situation. They are both aware that reality has been disturbed and perception upset. With the choices available, they are not very clear with which set of characters to engage. Surely the fawning, considerate and charming ideal family is far too good to be real, but they are much more comfortable to be with than the suburban, authentic alternative, when the real husband and sister-in-law eventually make their first drab appearance.

Five minutes with both families, one real and one imagined, has put the audience in the same dilemma as Susan. But Ayckbourn has done more than that. For when Susan cries 'Why have I gone to hell? ... I've tried so terribly hard, too. Terribly hard', he is outlining his dramatic theme. Susan's real world is no heaven, as she long ago realized. The vicarage comes very close to being some kind of hell. The Reverend Gerald Gannet, her husband, is a self-obsessed man in retreat from responsibility, dedicated to writing his history of the parish from the Middle Ages to the present day. But he is incapable of real affection for his wife, offering only empty pious platitudes. Muriel, his widowed sister, is *a woman who has known her share of suffering and is anxious others should know about it too'*, as Ayckbourn wittily puts it. She seeks reunion with her dead husband through spiritualist mumbo-jumbo. Susan's son has rejected his parents to become a member of some Trappist cult. But we quickly see that there is no consolation in any of these religious escape routes. Susan feels that each member of the household is avoiding proper human love in their own formularized self-interest, and by so doing they are the authors of her unhappiness.

At first we are very sympathetic, inclined to agree. And no wonder. The alternative family is so attractive; they are a picture of what Susan aspired to before sexual affection died between her and Gerald and with it any real companionship – even the gardening is a lonely chore now. Surely she has indeed tried so terribly hard to accept her role: playing the part of good cleric's wife, stepping in when Gerald found it impossible to tell Rick, their son, the sexual facts of life, putting up with Muriel's incompetent cooking which, alarmingly, includes omelettes 'fines herbes' made with Earl Grey tea.

But gradually it dawns upon both Susan and the audience that she might well be the author not only of her own unhappiness but also that of the other members of her family. Rick in particular, on a final visit home, contradicts her notion that it was Gerald who made life at home unbearable for him. Certainly Susan's attitude to sex seems unusually prim; we learn, for instance, that she could never consider undressing in front of her husband. Rick points out that hers is a personality no child could find comforting. 'I don't want to hurt you any more, Mum, but God help any daughter who had you as a mother.'

Meanwhile, Susan's alternative fantasy family may be no consolation after all. They start to make inconvenient appearances, interrupting at crucial moments and no longer playing a purely passive role. Worse, they seem to be acquiring sinister aspects. The bloody animal corpse hanging from the gun bag of Susan's perfect brother may be linked to the howling dog in the garden next door. The horrifying climax is sexual consummation with her idealized husband, at the height of which Susan realizes that she is making love to the Devil. Eventually, both real and idealized family come to be seen in a devilish incarnation conjoined in a lunatic social and ecclesiastical tableau.

The effect of this realization is intensified for the audience because Ayckbourn has fulfilled the ambition implicit in his initial stage directions. He has united audience and protagonist, making both see the world entirely from her viewpoint. The horror is that to the discomfort of the audience, and as a consequence of the completion of his stage direction, she slides into total insanity, the stage lit by the blue flashing light of an ambulance. As Ayckbourn says, the audience has 'thrown in its lot with someone who isn't altogether to be trusted, either in her opinions or her perceptions'.

In an interview about this play, he said, 'I wanted to write a first person narrative, a play seen, like a film, through the lens of a hand held camera. A play that would do the very thing one is careful to avoid as a dramatist. That is, break the rules, undermine normal logic, slowly rob the situation of reality.' He may indeed break rules in his ambition to blur the distinctions between film and theatre conventions. But it is no empty experiment; Ayckbourn always employs his mastery of technical skill, conventional or unorthodox, to enhance the fusion of theme with the means of delivery.

4

Facing Evil

'Oh my god, we're going under Armageddon Bridge.'
'It's OK, we'll be OK.'

These lines from *Way Upstream* (1981) point to a change of direction for Ayckbourn. The play describes the holiday cruise of a collection of friends who have hired a boat 'because', says Ayckbourn, 'a vast proportion of Britons are stupid enough to believe they come from a seafaring race' and surprisingly often 'go out on the Broads and ram each other'. We shall start at Pendon, the location for most of Ayckbourn's plays. This is his universal middle England; somewhere lying perhaps in Berkshire, a 'non-town', its chance of an individual personality swamped by too close a proximity to London but affording a prosperous middle-class comfort for most of its residents. It is his natural dramatic milieu, the ideal place to bring the lives and loves of theatre's middle-class audiences under the microscope. But we are warned clearly enough in the scene list that this play involves no ordinary location. The action is set on the River Orb, aboard the cabin cruiser *Hadforth Bounty*. We shall journey into Gessing Lock, pass through Stumble Lock, before ducking under Armageddon Bridge and emerging with an optimistic sense of freedom at the head of the river.

The voyage from realism to allegory was a daring departure for the playwright who had by 1981 established his credentials as a keen observer of the battlefields of marriage and small-town morality. But *Way Upstream* suffered at the hands of critics at the time of production, who generally saw it as technically overdemanding and morally ambivalent. Perhaps the most damaging of remarks came from a loyal and acute observer of the Scarborough output, Robin Thornber. Writing in his

Guardian review, he observed that 'philosophically, it's a plug for the soggy centrism of the Social Democratic Party'. It was a recognition that Ayckbourn had moved into new territory, that his purpose was larger than mere observation of domestic frailty. But, though at the time Thornber's remark linking this foray to political movements seemed apt and relevant, it was essentially a misunderstanding of the intent behind the allegory.

Ayckbourn had always studiously avoided political stances: 'Political theatre is usually so busy being political that it forgets to be theatre'. Indeed, he eschewed almost any opportunity to be judgemental about his characters or their situations. An author so firmly focused on the narrative line in both his plays and his directing had shown a reluctance to condemn even in his most ferociously unsympathetic characters. It is very hard to think of real villains in Ayckbourn's work before *Way Upstream*. Uncle Harvey, in *Season's Greetings* (1980), is dangerous, practically demented, but, as always, understandable. His disagreeable nature can be explained by his excluded position in the family. This is even clearer in the unpublished first script of the play, where his wife, an unseen, offstage, disgruntled heap, provides a presence to share a feeling of exclusion. The device proved unsatisfactory and was cut from the play in its later performances; Harvey became a more sinister character.

But, in *Way Upstream*, Vince and Fleur are portraits of a different kind. Vince wants his own way and is determined to seize the power to realize it, using any manipulative means whatsoever. Fleur is an accomplice rich enough to sidestep social norms and niceties. Both abuse hospitality, good nature and compromise to serve their own ends. Ayckbourn introduces them into a situation ripe for mutiny with its own implicit power vacuum. The holiday organized by Keith gets off to a rocky start when he is delayed by business. His wife, June, already dissatisfied in her marriage, is determined to suffer discomfort in anything but silence. His business partner, Alistair, is a willing second fiddle, the managerial emollient around Keith's auto-cratic boorishness. He and his own wife, Emma, are born compromisers and good-naturedly cope with all difficulties such as boarding in the dark and inhabiting the river boat's cramped quarters. But leaving the responsibilities of work behind is not going to be easy. The workers in the factory, which the cruise is

46

an escape from, are about to strike, and the daily reports from the river bank by Mrs Hatfield indicate a worsening situation.

It is clear that, for Keith, the hired boat *Hadforth Bounty* is to be an extension of his small business empire. Naturally he is going to be captain; he has after all got a manual, *River Cruising on the Orb*. He clearly feels that power is a matter of meritocracy, and, since he is in charge in the office, he should naturally be captain aboard the boat.

When Vince and Fleur hitch a ride, they soon dispossess him of his position. What we are to see is that power is really in the hands of the unscrupulous. Keith is left behind when it comes to its use and abuse; the newcomer's manipulation of power is as ruthless as Keith's was incompetent. Vince's technique is dazzling; a helpful manner turns into an autocratic assumption of control. His air of authority is reinforced by an apparent familiarity with bewildering nautical jargon. At first everyone is impressed. They welcome his certainties and June even finds them sexually seductive. At the end of the first act, Vince is able to throw the manual, *River Cruising on the Orb* overboard.

He has displaced Keith as captain of the ship, and rules with a malign and self-serving cruelty. All means are employed: nicknames are used, affectionately at first, but then as form of mockery; clearly defined roles become traps of subservience. The boat is turned into a mini kingdom, serving all of Vince's appetites. It is a power cruelly abused. With June reduced to a sexual slave, Alistair and Emma, the meek, reasonable but ineffectual compromisers, become the butts of all Vince's tauntings, suffering several humiliations but ending up marooned on an island and walking the plank.

They have no recourse but to fight back. This is against all their mild-mannered instincts. They act out of desperation and loyalty to each other. Alistair takes on Vince in a fight, and a combination of accident, good luck and brute force with a tin of baked beans results in tables being turned and an escape up the river in the *Hadforth Bounty*. As James Fenton has pointed out, Ayckbourn sacrifices the moral high ground: 'When it gets serious, it seems, inadvertently, to suggest that violence is a good thing'.

Nonetheless, Ayckbourn has taken an important thematic step, though it is not a political one. The plays from *Way Upstream* onwards are concerned more and more with a discussion of the abuse of power. He increasingly employs characters who wield power on a supra-domestic level and use it to malign purpose.

Behind this new discourse lies an assumption that power and evil are two sides of the same coin. Of course, this has been at the heart of his earlier domestic comedies, but characters such as Denis in *Just Between Ourselves* inadvertently wield power to cruel effect. They are pathetically flawed characters, victims of their own sense of inadequacy or motivated by misconceived good intentions, as Anthea and Richard are in *Joking Apart*.

But, having passed under Armageddon Bridge, we will begin to see Ayckbourn's guileless innocents upsetting the applecart of downright morally corrupt and evil personalities. The effect is to broaden the terms of reference. The new polarities in his plays are between society's manipulators of power and the victims of its abuse. As Billington has pointed out, Ayckbourn embarks, in plays after *Way Upstream*, on a discussion of the organs of power within late-twentieth-century Britain. In turn he examines the media, small and big business, local politics, science and medicine, and the church.

His dramatic milieux, though still familiar, are increasingly set outside Pendon. More and more alternatives to the domestic provincial household appear. Ayckbourn's mise-en-scène is transmuted into lavish villas on the Costa del Sol (*Man of the Moment*, 1988) over-themed ethnic restaurants (*Time of My Life*, 1992), and whole imaginary landscapes (*The Revengers' Comedies*, 1989). They even include futuristic households inhabited as much by robotic technology as human beings (*Henceforward...* 1997), and a number of Ayckbourn's plays for children. These are settings far removed from the living rooms and gardens of the early plays.

The new locations herald a discussion of larger issues. The plays retain their comic force, losing some of the bleakness of the plays of the seventies but sharpened by a moral and social irony. Ayckbourn has begun to write about the nature of evil in our society in his own way. There remains the focus on ordinary apolitical human beings who just wish to get on with their lives. The Scarborough playwright never loses his concern for the little man (or woman) and their desire for self-fulfilment in a domestic bliss. And his comic genre demands that the innocent can finally say 'It's OK, we'll be OK'.

Moral and political absolutists will sometimes find this less than satisfactory, but they are misunderstanding Ayckbourn. He is essentially a describer and arbiter, not a judgementalist. In this he is to be likened to two playwrights he cites as influences, Pirandello and Priestley. Like them he has experimented with chance and time, using both in constructing multi-pathed plays. As an accomplished technician, he seizes these elements as dramatic puzzles and theatrical opportunities. But they are more than that. What does emerge, as he uses time and chance in a series of plays, is a conviction that in life these two elements are catalysts in the forging of innocence or guilt.

In *Sisterly Feelings*, the tossing of a coin determines, at each individual performance, the action that follows. Depending on whether it's heads or tails, either Dorcas or Abigail walks home with Simon. The narrative splits into two alternative paths, dealing with either marital infidelity in Abigail's case, or a double-crossed affair for Dorcas. Further choices lie along the way for the sisters and, as Ayckbourn says, 'The whole device has the effect of stimulating actors, irritating stage managers, and infuriating box-office staff'. But his purpose is to question how much we really control our lives; do we make decisions or merely think we do. He claims he is no great believer in the inevitable fatalism of predestination, 'but I do believe that mostly we finish up with the friends and the partners in life that we deserve', 'If you don't like the person you end up married to it is probably your fault for being the sort of person you are'.

The idea is worked out at enormous length in *Intimate Exchanges* (1982) and the device is even more complex. The statistics are bewildering. Choices made by the characters/actors at the end of scenes produce sixteen possible endings and a total of thirty-one scenes each involving half a dozen characters played by two actors. The whole work is a piece of Byzantine dramatic architecture, a dazzling display of play-writing technique. But, again, as Billington says: 'If there is any one message to be deduced from these multi-layered, seemingly contradictory, extraordinarily rich plays, it is that the pattern of our lives is determined by a multitude of things and that the illusion of chance is balanced by the imperatives of character' (*Alan Ayckbourn*, London, 1983/1990).

The other great element that Ayckbourn has exploited is

dramatic time. It becomes not only a metaphor for real time but an alternative element to chance as a determiner of character. The most sustained development of this theme forms the action of *Time of My Life* (1992).

A family dinner starts the play. It is organized in a seedy restaurant of indeterminate ethnicity (the dishes include a pasta called 'crimpledoos', and a chocolate pudding called 'chooker') and is to celebrate the birthday of Laura, the wife of Gerry Stratton and mother of Glyn and Adam. Glyn's wife, Stephanie, and Adam's new girlfriend, Maureen, complete the group. At the end of the first scene the party breaks up, leaving the mother and father alone at the table. Subsequent scenes take place at three separate tables, where we see the three couples dining on occasions over a period of time. Ayckbourn's device is that, whilst Adam and Maureen's encounters take place at an increasingly early date each time we see them, Stephanie and Glyn's move forward in time from the night of the family dinner. We also discover that, though the parents sit at the same table for the duration of the play, they will leave the restaurant that night to be involved in a car crash resulting in Gerry's death.

At first sight the device is a typical Ayckbourn piece of play-writing wizardry – simple to achieve but complex in its perverse disruption of Aristotelian unities. There is much fun to be gained, particularly when we see Maureen and Adam's relationship 'progress' backwards to their eventual first encounter. Why, we wonder, do they sit in blank indifference while a singing foreign waiter performs a farcical folksong in excruciating style? In later scenes we see them relishing this performance and realize that this was an old act. They are grown indifferent to its charms when we first see them not enjoying it in the future. The grammatical difficulty of composing that last sentence emphasizes the complexity of the schema, and its perfection as a singularly dramatic device.

But this is no mere caprice. Its function is to explore the effect time has on our sense of self-definition. Both boys are under the forceful personality of their mother. She rules them and their father with a mixture of emotional blackmail and an imposing iron will. She has decided that Adam is a genius poet and is prepared to indulge his every artistic whim no matter how feckless he seems to his father. Glyn, she decides, is inadequate even to run the business alongside his father. His wife she tolerates only as a sycophantic appendage to her son.

By following the relationships of the two younger couples forwards and backwards in time from the evening when their father is killed and their mother hospitalized, we see the influence both malicious and benign of time. Maureen becomes less and less insecure in her relationship with Adam. Moving back in time, each scene reveals a more confident working-class girl who falls completely in love with a rich poet boy. We watch as the nervous, remoulded Maureen of the first scene becomes what she was when they first met, a confident, extrovert, punk youngster. We realize that time will strip her of this self-confidence, so joyously manifest in a variety of outrageous clothes and candy-coloured hairstyles, as she is brought nearer and nearer to meeting the formidable Laura. We see the relationship change as the action progresses from what we first see to something more innocent and beguiling. All the more shocking, then, to see once more, at the end of the play, the petrified, anxious doll moulded in a vain attempt to match Laura's expectations.

Glyn and Stephanie's scenes move forward in time and present a different perspective. The car crash and its tragic consequences precipitate a crisis in their marriage. At last the affair Glyn is conducting can be confronted by his wife without reference to his parents. His late nights cannot be explained only by his taking over the reins from his deceased father. We watch as Stephanie first goes into a decline of self-doubt and then emerges with a new-found confidence and self-realization. Glyn on the other hand goes from furtive deceiver to divorcee and then, abandoned by his mistress, he is left cast adrift, ironically fulfilling his mother's expectations.

And both changes effected by time are contrasted with middle-aged parents lingering at the table cluttered with the remnants of celebration. Gerry's toast which ends the play is loaded with irony. 'You know, in life, you get moments – just occasionally which you can positively identify as being among the happy moments. They come up occasionally, even take you by surprise, and sometimes you're so busy worrying about tomorrow or thinking about yesterday, that you tend to miss them altogether. I'd like to hope tonight might be one such moment.' Ayckbourn has contrived that we have already seen yesterday and tomorrow and can form our own judgement.

The pranks of time and chance go a long way to explaining Ayckbourn's attitude to the majority of his characters. His reluctance to judge them adds the bleakness to plays such as *Just Between Ourselves* and to the sustained elegiac last act of *Absurd Person Singular*. There is rarely a truly culpable person at the heart of these situations. For Ayckbourn, innocence or guilt is a result of the throw of the dice of chance, time and character. Blame is not his purpose as a playwright.

Until, that is, after *Way Upstream*, he looks outside his domestic battlegrounds and examines factors, institutions, organs of state which impinge on the lives of the meek and unassuming. There he finds characters to personify the malign effects of these forces. They emerge as epitomes of evil, to confront the ordinary man or woman and to use them as their plaything.

It is made quite clear, from the outset, in *Man of the Moment* (1988) that what Douglas Beechey has entered is a trap, engineered by ruthlessly ambitious media types, but manipulated by a vicious thug whose only real concern is his own self-seeking. The odious TV producer, Jill Rillington, is fronting her one big idea for a television programme with impact, *Their Paths Crossed*, and has brought together the two central protagonists in a bank raid which took place several years ago. Since then Vic Parks, the shotgun-carrying robber, has served time, written his autobiography and become a media celebrity with his own chat shows and, heaven help us, children's programme. The crime involved the taking of a hostage. She was wounded during a successful attempt to foil the thieves by a humble bank clerk, Mr Beechey. Douglas enjoyed the usual seven-day wonder of celebrity, marrying the hostage and having an annual bravery award named after him, but soon returned to obscurity. Until he is, once again, brought to confront Parks in his sumptuous Mediterranean villa.

This premise for the action has in it so many moral ambiguities and dilemmas that the following narrative is a minefield of dramatic and ethical ironies which Ayckbourn exploits to the full. And we are left in no doubt as to the moral judgement of the playwright. Jill Rillington is at her wits' end to make Beechey interesting in television terms, finding his humble Christian simplicity and forgiving nature entirely unsuited to television. 'Happy contented people are box office death, Douglas... and we really don't want to know about them. Not at all.' She and Parks's manager are ruthless enough to care more about a good television shot than rescuing a gardener drowning in the swimming pool.

But they are merely agents for the truly exploitative crook. 'What makes you really angry?' enquires Rillington of Douglas, at her wits' end to make the man take a stance in terms sufficiently extreme to make good journalism. 'I suppose evil, really', is his reply, 'I feel strongly about that....Only, it's often hard to recognise. But there's a lot of it about you know.' It is at this precise moment that Vic Parks appears, breezing easy bonhomie, clutching the hand of his little child and ready to distort facts and feelings before the camera for his admiring public.

Man of the Moment is a vivid indictment of the power of the media to act as a succubus. Television is a mighty tool, and, Ayckbourn implies, in the wrong hands invites its own abuse by the ambitious, the insecure, the exploitative and the ruthless. He shows us its victims misled by half-truths and distortions made in the name of televisual impact. There is the adoring fan, now a cruelly bullied nanny to Parks's children, the wife who knows the real personality of the vicious criminal but is forced to lead a life of lies, and the innocent star-struck audience member who is persuaded to be used as a prop in the further self glorification which lies at the heart of the process.

But Ayckbourn does not let any of us escape. The final scene is one of his best, for, in a technically adroit curtain call, he indicts all of us as accomplices in the television scam. We suddenly become not theatregoers but an invited studio audience, watching the filming of a re-enactment of the scenes we have just witnessed. But the facts have been changed for the cameras, and so have the actors. We see glamorous versions of the protagonists telling a sanitized and distorted version of the truth. As audience members, we are controlled in our responses by a bullying studio manager, Ashley Barnes. His invitation for the extra applause for the credit sequence is revealing. 'That's when all the names of people you've never even *heard* of, doing jobs you don't even know what they *are*, this is when their names go *racing* across the screen while you're busy putting the cat out and couldn't care less.' These are, we suppose, the 'ordinary' men and women of the world of television, not famous and not even recognized in any way except that we are to applaud their part in the conspiracy of lies we too have just participated in. 'Let's tell all the people at home what a really good time you've had and then, who knows, perhaps they'll believe that they've had a good one too. And we'll get a second series after all. All right?' The device is awesome, many layered; television is not only distorting what it shows us, but duping our responses. It is making the special worthless and the ordinary special, and all for the good of the television industry and its employees. The studio, it seems, is, even after his death, an apt home for the pure evil of Vic Parks.

One by one Ayckbourn has tackled areas of moral, political and religious vacuum. In *Woman in Mind*, Susan is as much let down by the inadequacies of the moral teaching and example of the Church of England, in the shape of her cleric husband, as she is by the mythical cast she surrounds herself with. Both conspire in her fall into insanity and are conjoined in a final dream sequence in which everyone is addressed as a devil or beelzebub. At one point Susan's fantasy husband appears in saturnine form. 'Oh dear God,' she cries, 'I'm making love with the devil.'

Henry Bell enters into a devilish pact with the fearsome Karen Knightly in *The Revengers' Comedies* (1989), little realizing the ruthlessness with which she will sweep through the world of multi-national big business, capitalizing on the moral ambiguities of some of its practices. Karen is sworn to wreak revenge on behalf of H. Bell, and we relish the defeat of the arch opportunist, Bruce Tick. But, having watched this with conspiratorial glee, it dawns upon us that this lady is not for turning. Her relentless pursuit of power and self-interest is fanatical to the point of perversity. Henry, who has found it impossible to keep his side of the pact with any pleasure, becomes aware of the evil of a truly power-hungry personality when allowed to enter a moral void.

There could scarcely be a more comprehensive picture of a world without a complete ethical foundation than that shown us in *A Small Family Business* (1987). It is not a world without a value system; it endorses absolutely the virtues of entrepreneurship with its emphasis on self-help, personal profit and individual fulfilment. But in the end it proves inadequate. The moral compromisers in the family draw Jack McCracken into their world of corruption; it is one which involves stealing, prostitution, drug dealing and murder. Driven almost entirely by materialistic hunger, in the play's final scene they offer a devastating theatrical image on the multiple set. In one room our 'hero' is conspiring with the mafia in drug trafficking whilst in another the family celebrates its unity of purpose. Upstairs in the bathroom, Jack's daughter, Samantha, is injecting heroin into her arm.

These plays are a long way from the early stumbling experiment of *Way Upstream*. They develop questions about the prevailing moral and ethical national mood through the medium of comedy and on an apparently domestic level.

But it is a mark of Alan Ayckbourn as a restless artistic spirit that he constantly challenges himself either technically or thematically. In *Wildest Dreams* (1991) another twist of emphasis seems to be emerging. If we are let down by our national institutions and culture, as the plays from 1981 to 1991 suggest, where is the ordinary man or woman to go for solace or comfort. *Wildest Dreams* explores the possibility that we are increasingly seeking an escape route in avoidance and through fantasy lives.

The four central players who gather around the game board to play a form of 'Dungeons and Dragons' are quickly revealed to us as people with inadequate personal lives. Seventeen-year-old Warren Wrigley uses a computer to 'update and upprogramme ... the parameters and random options' that dictate the rules of play. He huddles over his PC in the privacy of his attic bedroom which his unfortunate mother, whom he treats with maniacal mistrust and scorn, is never allowed to enter. Rick (Alice) Toller, a young woman of indeterminate sexuality, leaves her squalid basement bedsit in which her mother abandoned her several years ago, and joins the game. Stanley and Hazel Inchbrook host the evenings to blunt the effects of a barren, loveless marriage and unfulfilling jobs.

In the game, these hapless souls find new identities which mirror their own but make up for individual inadequacies. Antisocial Warren becomes Xenos, an alien in the world of humans; diffident Stanley is Alric, the confident leader; unassuming Hazel, the impetuous Idonia; and Rick is identified as the cross-gendered Herwin. The object of the game, significantly, like the object of their own lives, is to chase and root out evil, and each of them has a focus of fear or hatred.

But the real crisis comes when a well-meaning stranger joins them. Marcie, described by Ayckbourn as 'a completely new character' within his canon, is running away from a violent husband and seeks refuge in Rick's flat. She is uncomplicatedly sunny, offering a sympathetic ear and inspiring such trust that the players invite her to join in. She adopts the name of Novia and plays with relish. That evening, the game reaches such an intensity that thunderclaps and the sound of the devil's hooves are heard. It is a moment when all five are in such a heightened state that reality and fantasy merge. It is a crisis point; they will never again be able to separate the two with any great precision. For, as Ayckbourn points out, 'We exorcise our own little demon and another one comes up and threatens us' (interview with the author, 1997).

Marcie is not content to be a passive participant and starts almost immediately to change the rules. The effect is alarming. With reality even harder for the players to identify, they chase their own wild dreams, Marcie at the centre of them. For Warren, she becomes the perfect partner to a new character he is transforming into. He is so sure this is taking place that he wears a ski-mask which he tears off to show Marcie the changes. She of course can only see his usual spotty adolescent face. Rick fails to find happiness in the lesbian relationship she enters into with Marcie, discovering herself not to be the dominant partner but a meek recipient of orders from her love object. Stanley is infatuated with Marcie, eventually making a declaration of love which is cruelly spurned. Hazel, identifying Marcie as a threat to her marriage, enters into a return to childhood. It is a desperate attempt to keep her husband by making herself so dependent that Stanley must take care of her. In an alarming series of scenes, we see her retreat into infancy, nappy clad and blubbering incoherently.

Wildest Dreams is a daring play. It explores the modern phenomenon of our retreat, let down by society's social, political and moral structures, into escapist dreams. It marks Ayckbourn's freedom to pursue narrative lines beyond naturalism and into fantasy. He may claim that this is a result of his having written 'family plays' with their less constrained storylines. But this seems to be a liberation that he will continue to exploit and its subject will be escapist fantasy.

In *Things We Do for Love* (1997), Barbara is a successful schoolmistress with a very sorted out existence. She is capable and happy in both her professional and home life, and quite content. Until, that is, a visit by an old schoolfriend, Nikki, and her very attractive fiancé, Hamish. In that eternally inexplicable way, Barbara and Hamish fall head over heels in love and consummate it on her bed whilst Nikki is taking a bath. The result is turmoil in everybody's life as the decision to tell Nikki is faced. It will of course shatter the comfortable but soppy fantasy that her engagement to Hamish has become. And she is not the only one to have to face a disillusioning experience.

Was Barbara really content before the love thing, or is this ecstatic new relationship the delusion? Nikki's obsession with her idealized schooldays has turned sour now that the object of her schoolgirl crush can act so faithlessly. Hamish finds that coping with a love-tossed life can be to stagger helplessly from one complex situation to another. But most extraordinary of all is the revelation that Gilbert the postman, who lives in the basement, has harboured a secret fantasy of love for Barbara. She discovers that he has stolen items of her clothing and dresses in them to paint an erotic (not to say obscene) fresco, Sistine Chapel-like, on the ceiling of his flat. The fantasies are shattered one by one, ending with a disturbingly serious fight between Barbara and Hamish. They literally beat each other up. Of course the quarrel is patched up. But in a breathtaking theatrical coup, the final picture is of the couple reuniting in a warm embrace. However, they are so bruised that each cuddle ends with a wince and an apology.

Once again, the subject is the use of fantasy to cope with a situation that has no accepted social or moral guidelines. But the fantasy is more willingly entered into and, when dissolved, replaced by yet another personal demon, sometimes equally fantastical. This multi-layered theme is imitated in the setting required for the play. We see a section cut through the house. Above Barbara's living room is the bottom of the bedroom, allowing us to see only feet, a head lolling out of the bed in sexual ecstasy or the spiteful destruction of furniture and clothing by a disillusioned Nikki. Below the living room is the ceiling of Gilbert's basement flat. Here we see him dressed in Barbara's designer label frock, lying on his back painting his pornographic fantasy.

In tackling this subject with his new found structural freedom, Ayckbourn is reflecting, in both content and form, a reality recognizable to much of the theatregoing audience. This is the essence of his play writing. His fifty-three plays over thirty years have always reflected the political and social drifts that the ordinary man or woman is subject to, and done it by means both accessible and challenging. *Wildest Dreams* and *Things We Do for Love* are a long way from *Relatively Speaking* with its cosy surface and adulterous centre. But all are reflections of and challenges to social and artistic norms. This is what has made Alan Ayckbourn's comedic eye and technique continually relevant.

5

Sir Alan Ayckbourn

Alan Ayckbourn is a classic example of the theatrical apprentice who learned his trade 'on the job'. He went straight from school at the age of 18 into the theatre, eschewing any higher education in favour of lessons to be absorbed from working in the profession. He started out by joining productions with actors from the age of the Actor Manager; his first jobs were in the companies of Sir Donald Wolfit and Ernest Milton. With Wolfit he saw through the grand romantic acting style; what he learned, he says, was that 'theatre is entertainment'. He went on to work with prestigious directors of a number of repertory theatre companies: Frank Hauser at the Oxford Playhouse and Stephen Joseph in Scarborough and Stoke-on-Trent.

He was fortunate to enter the profession when the repertory movement and its managers were still profoundly committed to the nurturing of talent. The theatre was an industry like most at the time, which saw itself as having a responsibility for training its apprentices – actors, stage managers and writers. This responsibility was undertaken as a matter of course. With few theatre schools and no university drama departments, skills were passed on within the theatrical trade in much the same way that they had been for centuries. Talent was steered towards self-improvement and opportunity, the only relevant qualification being ambition and a will to work. It was a path trodden by Dion Boucicault, Noël Coward, Charlie Chaplin and many others.

In the Watson conversations of 1981, Ayckbourn claimed to have lots of Dryden and Chekhov on his shelves. Nowadays he is less inclined to talk about his intellectual influences and identify his mentors. Except of course for Stephen Joseph and his company. Ayckbourn is still quick to acknowledge his debt to that inspirational director and theorist. He has however no illusions. Joseph was not, he says, a great director, nor a particularly good organizer.

Looking back over the early Theatre in-the-Round work, the recorded repertoire betrays little. What emerges from a list of the plays done during Alan Ayckbourn's time there as an actor and stage manager is standard fare. There is the usual mix of classic play, recent West End hit, adaptation from a novel. There are also a number of new plays written by David Campton and many others. But the play list is no great literary resource. True, Strindberg's *Miss Julie* and Sartre's *Huis clos* precede Ayckbourn's own *Love After All*, and there are productions of *Hamlet*, *A Doll's House*, and *Arden of Faversham*. But this is only remarkable in so far as it is the repertoire of a seaside rep dedicated to entertaining a holiday audience. The apprentice author would find here the same influences he might in any large metropolitan company of the time. But of course he would be encouraged to find his own voice alongside that of Henry Livings, Alan Plater and Stan Barstow.

Harold Pinter came to Scarborough and, as Ayckbourn remembers, directed a production of his own *The Birthday Party*. 'That had a very strong effect. I think if you are to develop, you take these influences and they disappear into your bloodstream... If I did look like a poor man's Harold Pinter it would be dreadful... He has a love of distorting the everyday phrase, slightly bending it. He bends it more than I do. But I also bend phrases or put them into incongruous positions in speeches, which I hope makes them funny, because they seem slightly out of context.' Ayckbourn is right. One immediately thinks of Sidney Hopcroft in *Absurd Person Singular* saying, 'I've partitioned off part of the spare bedroom as a walk in cupboard for the wife', and Leslie Bainbridge in *Taking Steps* describing the members of his family firm: 'There's a B. Bainbridge, that's my brother Brian. An S. Bainbridge, who's my cousin Stu who's principally electrical...' These examples perhaps lack what Ayckbourn defines as Pinter's poetry, but they are every bit a match as inadvertent revelations of character.

Significantly, in the Scarborough play list from 1959 to 1969, there are a number of plays by Jean Anouilh, Luigi Pirandello and J. B. Priestley. 'I was very drawn to the craftsmen of the business', says Ayckbourn, and his attraction to these playwrights is interesting. 'I was very keen on Anouilh. I liked the way he constructed.' This penchant for the skill of the 'well made play' dogged both of these playwright/directors at a time when established play construction fell under suspicion. As Kalson notes, like Anouilh, Ayckbourn the craftsman for a long time enjoyed better responses from audiences than from critics.

He and Anouilh also share other characteristics: a fundamental theme – the incompatibility of man and woman locked into a relationship sanctioned by marriage – and, with it, a capacity to move unexpectedly between laughter and cruel truth. Both authors can evoke offstage, unseen characters who dominate the onstage action but remain conjured only in the audience's imagination (*Dinner with the Family* and *Absent Friends*). Both use the device of a play within a play to revelatory comic effect (*The Rehearsal* and *A Chorus of Disapproval*).

Like Priestley they are concerned with the corrosive effect of time and memory. One of Ayckbourn's most outstanding Scarborough productions was a revival of Priestley's *Time and The Conways*. This play juxtaposes past and present in alternate acts, highlighting the dashing of high expectations on the rocks of time, and the pernicious effect of choices and decisions. Priestley's work can be seen as an influence throughout Ayckbourn.

Above all, Alan Ayckbourn shares with Anouilh, Priestley and Pirandello an interest in the effect of theatricality on the narrative. All have used the theatre as a metaphor for life and all have played with the consequences of acknowledging the overlapping of fantasy and reality that is at the heart of both the human condition and the act of theatre.

Pirandello found a remarkable champion in England at the University of Leeds, where Frederick Bentley promoted his work assiduously through translations and productions in the late 1950s and early 1960s. If you were interested in theatre, and lived in Leeds at that time, you inevitably came across this zeal. In 1964 Alan Ayckbourn was invited by another Pirandello enthusiast, Alfred Bradley, to join BBC Radio North in Leeds as a drama producer. He remained there until 1970 but the effect of this period on his subsequent work remains underestimated.

Radio drama requires particular skills. The repertoire has always included classic pieces and new plays, aimed at a large audience and one which we can surely recognize as the natural constituency of the Ayckbourn canon. The plays are often concerned with domestic situations and issues of contemporary familiarity. The director of radio drama understands the importance of narrative and relies on dialogue for character drawing. Ayckbourn's apparently naturalistic but finely tuned conversations, and his emphasis, as both author and director, on narrative clarity, may well owe something to this experience.

What these influences and training gave Alan Ayckbourn was the technical craftsmanship that he so admired and which he exploited through his chosen genre of comedy. His output forms a bridge between the Comedy of Manners of the early part of the century and that of the eighties and nineties. He started by aping Coward and Douglas-Home, setting his early work in the drawing rooms of a comfortable upper middle class. But Ayckbourn draws upon a different range of social types and settings to that which had previously been exploited. He moved quickly from neat 'stockbroker-belt' home to the untidy atmospheres of redbrick housing estates (*How the Other Half Loves* juxtaposes both milieux onstage simultaneously). His plays are set in the 1960s–70s housing estates, the interwar semis and the decaying Victorian suburbs that represent home for the larger part of his audiences.

His move down the collective scale into more modest environments reflects the social development of the sixties and seventies. But his concern is not largely political and he therefore stops short of the working-class territory so vividly exploited by D. H. Lawrence and the Manchester School – including Harold Brighouse, W. S. Houghton – in the early part of the century, and in the fifties by Keith Waterhouse and Willis Hall, Bill Naughton and Shelagh Delaney. His plays are not 'peeping Tom' exercises in social realism but comedy of manners that reflects the growth of the middle class and the strains and tensions inherent in comfortable conformity.

Alan Ayckbourn championed the cause of comedy in the theatre against the counterclaim by television for the audience's attention. His influence on the television sitcom is easily demonstrable (*The Good Life* and its cast grew out of *The Norman Conquests*) but more important is the ground he claimed for playwrights such as Alan Bleasdale, Willie Russell and John

Godber. He had persuaded an audience, who could more easily find entertainment in their own homes, of the value of the theatre as an expression of their reality. The younger playwrights readily exploited this, taking their cue from Ayckbourn by focusing on the lives of their audience and placing entertainment at the heart of their work. He had continually challenged the conventional form of theatre and each of these playwrights owes much of the filmic quality of their scripts to him.

Epilogue

In 1997, for services to the theatre, Her Majesty Queen Elizabeth II bestowed upon the playwright who has for thirty years written plays for the Theatre-in-the-Round, Scarborough, the title of Sir Alan Ayckbourn.

Letter to the Scarborough Evening News, 12 December 1996

> *Dear Sir,*
> *It's high time Alan Ayckbourn and his ilk realised that not many people, rightly or wrongly, want to watch live theatre and if he still insists Scarborough should have a theatre, then let him pay for it as the rest of us have to do.*
> *Otherwise close it down. It's obvious that not many people want it. The council can close toilets, lighthouses, to keep the place going.*
> *Just what do you think you are doing with our money, councillors?*

Select Bibliography

WORKS BY AYCKBOURN

Plays

Listed chronologically by date of first performance.

The Square Cat (1959).
Love After All (1959).
Dad's Tale (1960).
Standing Room Only (1961).
Xmas v. Mastermind (1962). A children's play.
Mr Whatnot (1963).
Relatively Speaking (1965), originally *Meet My Father.*
The Sparrow (1967).
How the Other Half Loves (1969).
Me Times Me Times Me (1970). Retitled *Family Circles.*
Time and Time Again (1971).
Absurd Person Singular (1972).
*The Norman Conquests: Table Manners: Living Together: Round and Round the
    Garden* (1973). Trilogy of three full-length plays.
Absent Friends (1974).
Confusions (1974).
Bedroom Farce (1975).
Just Between Ourselves (1976).
Ten Times Table (1977).
Joking Apart (1978).
Sisterly Feelings (1979). Two interlocking plays.
Taking Steps (1979).
Suburban Strains (1980). With Paul Todd – a musical play.
Season's Greetings (1980).
Way Upstream (1981).
Making Tracks (1981). With Paul Todd – a musical play.
Intimate Exchanges (1982–3). Eight interlocking plays.

A Trip to Scarborough (1982). With Paul Todd, adapted from R. B. Sheridan – a play with music.

It Could Be Anyone One of Us (1983).

A Chorus of Disapproval (1984).

Woman in Mind (1985).

A Small Family Business (1987).

Henceforward… (1987).

Man of the Moment (1988).

Mr A's Amazing Maze Plays (1988). A children's play.

The Revengers' Comedies (1989). Two sequential plays.

Invisible Friends (1989).

Body Language (1990).

This Is Where We Came In (1990).

Callisto 5 (1990). A children's play.

Wildest Dreams (1991).

My Very Own Story (1991).

Time of My Life (1992).

Dreams from a Summer House (1992). With John Pattison – a musical play.

Communicating Doors (1994).

Haunting Julia (1994).

The Musical Jigsaw Play (1994). With John Pattison – a children's play with music.

A Word from our Sponsor (1995). With John Pattison - a play with music.

By Jeeves (1996). With Andrew Lloyd Webber – a musical play.

The Champion of Paribanou (1996). A children's play.

Things We Do for Love (1997).

Comic Potential (1998).

Miscellaneous – Revues, Short Plays, One-Act Plays

Follow the Lover/Double Dutch (unpublished). Reviews.

Mixed Doubles (1969). A one-act play in a collection of five by various authors.

Ernie's Incredible Illucinations (1969). A short children's play.

Service Not Included (1974). A review.

Men on Women on Men (with Paul Todd) (1978). A review.

First Course/Second Helping (1980). With Paul Todd – a review.

Me, Myself and I (1981). With Paul Todd – a revue.

Incidental Music (1983). With Paul Todd – a review.

A Cut in the Rates (1983). A short play.

The Seven Deadly Virtues (1984) A review.

The Westwoods (1984).

Boy Meets Girl (1985). With Paul Todd – a revue.

Girl Meets Boy (1985). With Paul Todd – a revue.

Mere Soup Songs (1986). With Paul Todd – a revue.
The Inside Outside Slide Show (1989). A short play.

Collections

Most of the plays are published separately by Samuel French Ltd., or by Faber and Faber. A few are collected in editions; they are:

Joking Apart and Other Plays (Penguin, 1982). Also contains *Just Between Ourselves, Ten Times Table, Sisterly Feelings.*
The Norman Conquests (Chatto and Windus, 1977; Penguin, 1979).
Three Plays (Chatto and Windus, 1977; Penguin, 1979). Contains *Bedroom Farce, Absurd Person Singular, Absent Friends.*

Articles by Ayckbourn

'Alan Ayckbourn' (lecture) *Drama*, 1 (1988), 5–7.
'Provincial Playwriting', *The Author*, 81 (Spring 1970), 25–8.
'A Westwood Diary', 22–page article in programme 'Celebrating 25 Years at Westwood' for production of *Just Between Ourselves*, 1996.

CRITICAL AND BIOGRAPHICAL STUDIES

Alan Ayckbourn used to pride himself that he was one of the least written about playwrights. It was true that there are few major books on his plays, but he is served very well by the following.

Almansi, Guido, 'Victims of Circumstance: Alan Ayckbourn's Plays', in *Encounter*, April 1978, pp. 58–65; repr. in John Russell Brown (ed.) *Modern British Dramatists: New Perspectives* (Englewood Cliffs, NJ: Prentice Hall, 1984), 109–20.
Billington, Michael, *Alan Ayckbourn*; Macmillan Modern Dramatists, (Macmillan, 1983/1990).
Blistein, Elmer M., 'Alan Ayckbourn: Few Jokes Much Comedy', in *Modern Drama*, 26 (March 1983), 26–35.
Dukore, Bernard F. (ed), *Alan Ayckbourn: A Casebook* (Garland Publishing, 1991).
Hobson, Harold, 'Alan Ayckbourn: Playwright of Ineradicable Sadness', *Drama*, Winter 1982, pp. 4–6.
Kalson, Albert E., *Laughter in the Dark: The Plays of Alan Ayckbourn* (Associated University Press, 1993).
Nightingale, Benedict, *An Introduction to 50 Modern British Plays* (Pan Books, 1982).
Page, Malcolm (ed.), *File on Ayckbourn* (March 1989).

Taylor, John Russell, *Anger and After: A Guide to the New British Drama* (Methuen, 1962).

Taylor, John Russell, *The Second Wave: British Drama for the Seventies* (Hill and Wang, 1971).

Watson, Ian, *Alan Ayckbourn: Bibliography, Biography, Playography*; Theatre Checklist No. 21 (TQ Publications, 1980).

Watson, Ian, *Conversations with Ayckbourn* (Macdonald, 1981).

White, Sidney Howard, *Alan Ayckbourn*; Twayne English Authors (Boston, MA; G. K. Hall, 1984).

Index